Presented to:

From:

ZONDERKIDZ

The Beginner's Bible® 365 Devotions for Kids
Copyright © 2011, 2015 by Zonderkidz
Illustrations © 2005, 2016, 2017 by Zonderkidz
Previously published as *The Beginner's Bible Kid-Sized Devotions*

Published in Grand Rapids, Michigan, by Zonderkidz. Zonderkidz is a registered trademark of The Zondervan Corporation, L.L.C., a wholly owned subsidiary of HarperCollins Christian Publishing, Inc.

Requests for information should be addressed to customercare@harpercollins.com.

ISBN 978-0-310-76306-2

Illustrations: Denis Alonso
Design: Cindy Davis

Printed in Canada

24 25 26 27 28 29   MAR   12 11 10 9 8 7

365 Devotions
for Kids

Previously titled
The Beginner's Bible Kid-Sized Devotions

Spending time with God is important to us as Christians. There is no better thing to do when you are filled with joy or sadness, anger or contentment. This is what we need to teach our children! To understand that thinking, praying, and talking to God is key to strengthening and growing their faith.

Who better to ask?
Who better to praise?
Who better to thank,
than the Lord Almighty?

In the beginning, God created the heavens and the earth.
—Genesis 1:1

Day 1

God had his angels with him in heaven. And he was happy. But he wanted to share. He had a plan to create the world and everything on it and in it. This is so long ago, but he knew it was a good plan and he got started.

God wanted something more. He wanted to share. God wanted to love, so he had a plan.

Thank you, God, for everything.

The earth didn't have any shape. And it was empty.
—Genesis 1:2

Day 2

Only God can make something out of nothing! That is how he made the world.

God wanted to make the world. And he did it! It is amazing that he made it all out of nothing. Think about how hard it would be for you to make something out of nothing. It is impossible for you. But it is not impossible for God!

Thank you, God, for creating the world!

And that's exactly what happened. God made the huge space between the waters. He separated the water under the space from the water above it. God called the huge space "sky." There was evening, and there was morning ... —Genesis 1:7–8

Day 3

God has a great imagination. He thought up every part of creation all by himself. He wanted to make things that made him happy. He had a plan to make people, and his creation would make them happy too.

God created everything by himself. No one had to tell God how to do it.

Thank you, God, for your great imagination!

God said, "Let the water under the sky be gathered into one place. Let dry ground appear." And that's exactly what happened. God called the dry ground "land." He called all the water that was gathered together "seas." And God saw that it was good. —Genesis 1:9–10

Day 4

God just has to say the word and things are created!

God has great power. He knew what he wanted to create and so he did it! And the creations he made were just the way he thought they should be. Everything worked and fit into the world he was making.

Thank you, God, for all you made for us.

Then God said, "Let the land produce plants. Let them produce their own seeds. And let there be trees on the land that grow fruit with seeds in it. Let each kind of plant or tree have its own kind of seeds." And that's exactly what happened. —Genesis 1:11

Day 5

It was God's idea to make things in the world have color. He chose to make the sun yellow, the grass green, and the sky blue. Imagine what the world would be like if it were only black and white!

When God made heaven and earth, he made things colorful.

Thank you, God, for making the world a colorful place!

So God created the great sea creatures. He created every kind of living thing that fills the seas and moves about in them. He created every kind of bird that flies. And God saw that it was good.
—Genesis 1:21

Day 6

God created every kind of living creature.

Think about all the different kinds of living creatures. There is not just one kind of bird or one kind of fish! God thought them all up. Would you have been able to think of thousands of kinds of birds or fish like God did?

Thank you, God, for making so many types, shapes, and sizes of creatures!

*God made every kind of wild animal. He made every kind
of livestock. He made every kind of creature that moves
along the ground. And God saw that it was good.*
—Genesis 1:25

Day 7

Think about your favorite animal. God was the first to think of that animal. He came up with the idea for dogs and cats, elephants and turtles. God knew his creation of animals was good. He knew we would love them. He wants us to promise to care for them.

Animals have not always been around. God is the one who made them!

Thank you, God, for my pets and for all animals.

So God created human beings in his own likeness. He created them to be like himself. He created them as male and female.
—Genesis 1:27

Day 8

God's best creation was people!

People have not been around forever. God created man and woman. He designed them and gave them life. Think about all the people you know. Every one of them is different. And every one of them is special to God.

Thank you, God, for making me just the way I am!

*Then the LORD God formed a man. He made him out
of the dust of the ground. God breathed the breath of life
into him. And the man became a living person.*
—Genesis 2:7

Day 9

God made everything. But his most wonderful creation is man. He had to think up brains and hearts and skin and muscles and even fingernails. God even thought up the senses like taste and smell and touch.

> God made man out of the dust of the earth. That is amazing!

Thank you, God, for creating man in your image.

The L<small>ORD</small> God had planted a garden in the east in Eden.
He put in the garden the man he had formed.
—Genesis 2:8

Day 10

God gave man a beautiful garden to live in. He didn't have to do that!

The Garden of Eden was great! It had everything people needed to live—food, water, animal friends, and God was there too! He knew exactly what man needed.

Thank you, God, for giving me everything I need.

The LORD God put the man in the Garden of Eden.
He put him there to farm its land and take care of it.
—Genesis 2:15

Day 11

God wanted Adam to take care of creation. He wanted Adam to name the animals. He wanted Adam to feed them. He wanted Adam to grow food for every creature that needed it. He taught Adam how to work.

God gave Adam a job to do. He has a job for each one of us.

Thank you, God, for making us an important part of your creation.

The LORD God gave the man a command. He said, "You can eat fruit from any tree in the garden. But you must not eat the fruit of the tree of knowledge of good and evil."
—Genesis 2:16–17

Day 12

God told Adam and Eve not to eat from one tree in the garden.

God wants what is best for us. He wants to protect us from things that could be bad for us. Whenever God tells us not to do something, it is for a good reason.

Thank you, God, for protecting me.

The serpent was more clever than any of the wild animals the LORD God had made. The serpent said to the woman, "Did God really say, 'You must not eat the fruit of any tree in the garden'?"
—Genesis 3:1

Day 13

Satan is a bad guy. He does not love God. He disguised himself as a snake. He had a plan to hurt God. He planned on using Adam and Eve to help him. Adam and Eve did not know about Satan.

God has an enemy. The enemy's name is Satan. He is also called the devil. You cannot trust him.

Thank you, God, for protecting me from Satan.

The woman said to the serpent, "We may eat the fruit of the trees in the garden. But God did say, 'You must not eat the fruit from the tree in the middle of the garden. Do not even touch it. If you do, you will die.'"
—Genesis 3:2–3

Day 14

The devil tricked Eve into doing something wrong and disobeying God.

Has anyone ever tried to get you to do something bad? God and your parents are always watching out for you. They love you and want you to be safe. They want you to always do what is right.

Thank you, God, for always watching over me.

The woman saw that the tree's fruit was good to eat and pleasing to look at. She also saw that it would make a person wise.
—Genesis 3:6

Day 15

God gave Adam and Eve the beautiful garden. They loved to look at everything God gave them. They were curious just like we are. But we remember something very important. God knows what is good for us. We need to believe God if he says something is not good.

Things that look good are not always good for you.

I believe in you, God.

Then both of them knew things they had never known before.
—Genesis 3:7

Day 16

Adam and Eve could not hide their bad choice from God. We cannot hide our bad choices either.

When Adam and Eve ate the fruit, something happened! Because they were told not to eat it and they did, God was very unhappy. The serpent had lied to them. It was not good knowledge they got after eating from the Tree of Knowledge.

God, I will be open and honest with you.

The man said, "It was the woman you put here with me.
She gave me some fruit from the tree. And I ate it."
—Genesis 3:12

Day 17

God gave Adam and Eve everything they needed. But they wanted more. When anyone gets more things, they have to take responsibility for that. God made sure that Adam, Eve, and Satan understood that.

When we do something bad, we are responsible. It does not help to blame someone else.

Thank you for helping me learn right from wrong.

23

Day 18

There are consequences when we do wrong, just like there were for Adam and Eve.

Adam and Eve made the wrong choice and listened to the serpent. God was angry and very disappointed. God had to teach them that they need to follow the rules. And so Adam and Eve had to leave the Garden. This made Adam and Eve sad.

Thank you for being willing to teach me.

So the LORD God drove the man out of the Garden of Eden to work the ground he had been made from.
—Genesis 3:23

Day 19

God sees and know everything. We cannot hide anything from God! He even knows what we are thinking and feeling. When we do something bad God knows it. But it is important to always remember that God never stops loving us, even when we do something bad.

God knows when we disobey him.

Thank you, God, for knowing everything and still loving me.

Day 20

When the people started to disobey God, he came up with a plan.

So many people were not following God. God was sad that he had even created humans! He had been so happy with them. He had said they were good! But no more. He decided that something had to be done to fix things on earth.

If I need fixing, please know I am ready, God.

Then the LORD said to Noah, "Go into the ark with your whole family. I know that you are a godly man among the people of today."
—Genesis 7:1

Day 21

God saw all the people on earth being bad. He knew he had to do something to stop all the bad. God had a plan. He knew that Noah was a good man, so God asked Noah to help him.

> God loves people. Noah was one of God's very special people on earth.

Thank you, God, for having a plan!

"So make yourself an ark out of cypress wood.
Make rooms in it. Cover it with tar inside and out."
—Genesis 6:14

Day 22

Sometimes the jobs God gives us to do are hard work!

Loving God is not always easy. Sometimes God wants us to do big, hard jobs. God knew a man named Noah. Noah love God. God knew that whatever he asked Noah to do, even if it was very hard, he would do it!

God, give me strength to do hard work for you!

"Two of every kind of bird will come to you. Two of every kind of animal will also come to you. And so will two of every kind of creature that moves along the ground. All of them will be kept alive with you."
—Genesis 6:20

Day 23

God asked Noah to do a big job. God knew it would be hard. But he made sure Noah had all the right tools. He made sure Noah had all the right supplies. God wanted Noah to be successful on the ark just like he wants us to be successful in the jobs he gives us.

> **God makes sure we have whatever we need to do his work.**

Thank you, God, for giving me the right tools to be successful.

*Pairs of all living creatures that breathe
came to Noah and entered the ark.*
—Genesis 7:15

Day 24

**Noah trusted
God to help him.**

Noah followed God's plan. He built an ark. God said to put two of every kind of animal into the ark, but how were all the animals going to get there? Noah trusted God, and when the time came, God sent the animals to Noah.

Thank you, God, for helping Noah out!

*"Seven days from now I will send rain on the earth. It will rain
for 40 days and 40 nights. I will destroy from the face
of the earth every living creature I have made."*
—Genesis 7:4

Day 25

God told Noah when it was time to load the ark. He gave Noah good directions. He made sure Noah understood them. God wants us to love and serve him the best way we know how. He never wants us to fail.

God sometimes gives us warning of things to come. He does not want us to fail!

I want to be a good believer, God!

Noah was 600 years old. It was the 17th day of the second month of the year. On that day all of the springs at the bottom of the oceans burst open. God opened the windows of the skies.
—Genesis 7:11

Day 26

God watches over us during both the calm times and the stormy times of life.

God helped Noah prepare, and when the rains came, God made sure Noah was ready. He made sure that the animals and Noah's whole family had what they needed to live in the ark. God's plan was working. He was taking care of his people.

Thank you, God, for taking care of me all the time.

The waters flooded the earth for 150 days.
—Genesis 7:24

Day 27

Noah, his family, and the animals on the ark waited and waited and waited. They were on the ark for many, many days. But God knew what he was doing. He gave them all strength. He gave them what they needed to live.

God has perfect timing for all things. Waiting is not always easy.

Lord, help me be patient.

He waited seven more days. Then he sent out the dove again from the ark. In the evening the dove returned to him. There in its beak was a freshly picked olive leaf! So Noah new that the water on the earth had gone down.
—Genesis 8:10–11

Day 28

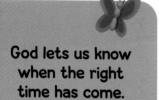

God lets us know when the right time has come.

When the rain was finally done falling, Noah needed to know. And God made sure Noah got the message. When it was the right time for Noah to leave the ark, God had a dove bring a branch back. The time to leave the ark had come!

Thank you for the many signs of your love, God.

So God said to Noah, "The rainbow is the sign of my covenant.
I have made my covenant between me and all life on earth."
—Genesis 9:17

Day 29

It rained for 40 days and 40 nights. It seemed like the rain would never stop. When the rain stopped, Noah prayed, "Thank you, God!" God said he would never again flood the whole world. He gave us rainbows to remind us of his promise.

When God makes a promise, he always keeps the promise!

Thank you, God, for rainbows and your promises!

But the Lᴏʀᴅ came down to see the city and the tower the people were building.
—Genesis 11:5

Day 30

No one on earth is bigger, better, or smarter than God.

After the flood, things changed on earth. God helped the people start over again, but the people became too sure of themselves. They thought they knew better than God! No one knows better than God! So God kept an eye on his people.

God, keep an eye on me when I begin to wander away from you.

Then they said, "Come on! Let's build a city for ourselves. Let's build a tower that reaches to the sky. We'll make a name for ourselves."
—Genesis 11:4

Day 31

After the flood, the people started to forget how much they needed God. They got together to build a tower to reach heaven. But it was not what God wanted! God wanted the people to follow his plans. He didn't want them to do things without him.

God wants us to love him and to need him.

Thank you, God, that you want us to need you.

So the LORD scattered them from there over the whole earth. And they stopped building the city.
—Genesis 11:8

Day 32

God knows what is best for us.

God knew that if the people built their big tower, they would think they could do anything all by themselves. But God wanted people to always need him! So God scattered the people all over the world and gave them different languages.

Thank you, God, for doing what is best for us.

The LORD had said to Abram, "Go from your country, you people and your father's family. Go to the land I will show you."
—Genesis 12:1

Day 33

God had a special friend named Abraham. Abraham was married to Sarah. They loved God and each other. They prayed to God often and God knew them well. God had an idea on how to say thank-you to Abraham for his great love and trust.

There are many special people that love and trust God no matter what. We can learn from them.

Let my love and trust for you grow like Abraham's, God.

So Abram went, just as the LORD had told him.
—Genesis 12:4

Day 34

God chose
Abraham
for a special job.

God talked to Abraham. He told him to pack up and go to a new land. Abraham did it! He took his wife and his nephew with him. He did not ask questions, he just trusted God.

Thank you, God, that I can trust you.

*"I will make you into a great nation. And I will bless you.
I will make your name great. You will be a blessing to others."*
—Genesis 12:2

Day 35

God blessed Abraham because of his faith. God was so proud of him! God promised Abraham a big family and lots of land. God rewarded Abraham because he believed in God and he believed God's promises.

God was happy that Abraham believed his promises.

Thank you, God, for your many promises to us.

Day 36

God can do anything. Even if it seems impossible, God can do it!

Abraham and Sarah were very old. But God said they would have a son! Sarah was so surprised that she laughed. She was nervous but happy. Could God really give them a son? Yes! God did it. It was a miracle!

Thank you, God, for your miracles!

By that time Abraham was very old.
The LORD had blessed Abraham in every way.
—Genesis 24:1

Day 37

Abraham always followed God's plan. He raised his son Isaac to love God. Isaac was a part of God's plan too ... the plan to have Abraham be the father of God's people. So when Isaac was grown up, Abraham knew that whatever God told him to do with Isaac, he needed to do it.

God's plan to have Abraham's family grow big and strong did not stop. God's plan for us never ends either.

Thank you, God, for making me part of your family.

And he married Rebekah. She became his wife, and he loved her.
—Genesis 24:67

Day 38

God leads people when they pray!

It was time for Isaac to get married. His dad, Abraham, sent a servant to look in his hometown for a nice girl who believed in God. The servant prayed for God to lead him. Sure enough, the servant met Rebekah. She was just the right one!

Thank you, God, for leading us when we pray.

But Isaac said, "Your brother came and tricked me. He took your blessing."
—Genesis 27:35

Day 39

Sometimes we want something so much that we will do anything to get it. But if we do something wrong, we will suffer for it. God wants us to make good choices and to do things the right way.

> **The choices we make are very important.**

Thank you, God, for helping me to be honest.

Day 40

Our choices can affect others and our future.

When we make bad choices, God still loves us. He will forgive us if we say we are sorry. But sometimes other people are not as quick to forgive us. They might be really mad! We should tell them if we are sorry.

Thank you, God, that you forgive me when I ask.

*"I am with you. I will watch over you everywhere you go.
And I will bring you back to this land. I will not leave you
until I have done what I have promised you."*
—Genesis 28:15

Day 41

Jacob had a dream. He saw a stairway with angels going up and down on it! Then God talked to him in the dream! God told Jacob that he would be with Jacob and watch over him wherever he went. God would bless Jacob and help him.

God talks to us in many ways!

Thank you, God, for talking to us.

*Jacob woke up from his sleep. Then he thought,
"The LORD is surely in this place. And I didn't even know it."
—Genesis 28:16*

Day 42

God is there even
when we don't
know it.

When Jacob woke up, he was
so happy. God had talked to him
in his dream and he had seen
angels! Jacob thanked God. He
said, "God is in this place, and
I didn't know it!" We should
remember that God is with us
even when we don't see him.

Thank you, God, for always being with me!

"They will be like the dust of the earth that can't be counted."
—Genesis 28:14

Day 43

God promised Jacob some wonderful things. God said he would give Jacob so many children and such a big family that Jacob would not be able to count them all! God said he would give Jacob the land he was lying on. God kept his promises.

God takes every promise he makes seriously.

Thank you, God, for your goodness!

But Esau ran to meet Jacob. He hugged him and threw his arms around his neck. He kissed him, and they cried for joy.
—Genesis 33:4

Day 44

God helps us fix broken friendships.

God wants us to get along with other people. It is not always easy. Sometimes we fight with brothers or sisters or friends. We get mad at people, and they get mad at us. God wants us to love each other. He can help us mend broken friendships.

Thank you, God, for helping me be nice to people.

God said to him, "I am the Mighty God. Have children so that there will be many of you. You will become the father of a nation and a community of nations. Your later family will include kings."
—*Genesis 35:11*

Day 45

God loved Jacob. God knew Jacob was faithful. Jacob was part of God's family, and God wants his family to grow and grow! He knew that Jacob would help teach his family members about God's love, just like our parents do.

> **God told Jacob to be faithful and multiply. God wants many people to be in his family!**

God, bless my family.

Israel loved Joseph more than any of his other sons.
That's because Joseph had been born to him when he was old.
Israel made him a beautiful robe.
—Genesis 37:3

Day 46

God does not
have favorites.

Joseph was Jacob's favorite son. Jacob made a colorful robe for Joseph. He wanted Joseph to feel special. Did you know that each and every one of us is very, very special to God? God loves all of his children very much. God does not have a favorite like Jacob did.

Thank you, God, for loving each one of us so very much!

Joseph had a dream. When he told it to his brothers, they hated him even more. He said to them, "Listen to the dream I had."
—Genesis 37:5

Day 47

Joseph had some strange dreams. He told his brothers about one dream. The dream made it sound like Joseph believed he was better than his brothers. The brothers were not happy about the dream. Why would this little boy have such a dream?

God speaks to his people in different ways. Sometimes he speaks through people's dreams.

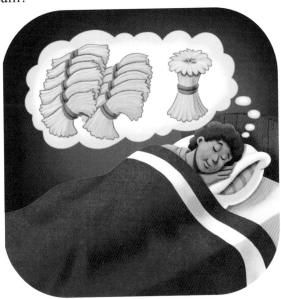

God, help me listen closely to your words.

His brothers said to him, "Do you plan to be king over us? Will you really rule over us?" So they hated him even more because of his dream. They didn't like what he had said.
—Genesis 37:8

Day 48

We should think about other people's feelings.

Sometimes brothers get angry at brothers. Sometimes they do not listen very well to each other. And sometimes they do not really care. Joseph told his brothers about his dream and they thought he was bragging. The brothers were not happy.

God, open my heart to how others feel.

And they threw him into the well. The well was empty.
There wasn't any water in it.
—Genesis 37:24

Day 49

Without even understanding the whole story, Joseph's brothers decided to do something wrong. They did something that could hurt their little brother Joseph! No one even took time to talk to Joseph about the problem!

Sometimes people will dislike us unfairly.

God, help me be forgiving to those who dislike me.

*When Joseph came to his brothers, he was wearing
his beautiful robe. They took it away from him.*
—Genesis 37:23

Day 50

God made families.
Everyone in a
family is special.

Joseph's big brothers were very angry at him. They didn't like his robe. They didn't like his dreams. They did not want him to be special. So they chose to do a very mean thing. They threw Joseph into a pit. They forgot that each of them were special too.

Thank you, God, that we are all special!

The traders from Midian came by. Joseph's brothers pulled him up out of the well. They sold him to the Ishmaelite traders for eight ounces of silver. Then the traders took him to Egypt.
—Genesis 37:28

Day 51

Joseph was sold and became a slave. This was not what he wanted. But God had a plan. He knew that from this bad thing in Joseph's life, something good would happen. God stays with us even when something in our life changes or goes wrong.

> If God lives in you, then he goes with you wherever you go.

Thank you, God, for staying with me no matter what!

So he put Joseph in prison. It was the place where the king's prisoners were kept. While Joseph was there in the prison, the L<small>ORD</small> was with him. He was kind to him. So the man running the prison was pleased with Joseph. —Genesis 39:20–21

Day 52

When Joseph was in prison, God showed Joseph his love.

Even when things did not look good for Joseph, God made sure he was fine. Joseph was in jail and God was there beside him. He helped Joseph make friends. God protected him and helped things work out for Joseph.

God, help me to remember that you are near.

"But when everything is going well with you, remember me.
Do me a favor. Speak to Pharaoh about me. Get me out of this prison."
—Genesis 40:14

Day 53

When Joesph was in jail, he met a man. The man was a wine tester for Pharaoh. Joseph helped the man by telling him what his dreams meant. Joseph's new friend left jail to go back to work for the Pharaoh. Joseph stayed in jail awhile longer.

God brings people into our life for a special reason. He always knows what we need.

Thank you, God, for knowing what I need.

The ugly, skinny cow ate up the seven cows that looked healthy and fat. Then Pharaoh woke up.
—Genesis 41:4

Day 54

God cares about people who don't know him.

God wanted Pharaoh to know him. God also wanted to warn Pharaoh about a time coming when there would be no food. God wanted to save people's lives! So God sent Pharaoh a bad dream. God knew that Joseph would be able to help Pharaoh understand his dream.

You are a great and caring God.

So Pharaoh sent for Joseph. He was quickly brought out of the prison. Joseph shaved and changed his clothes. Then he came to Pharaoh.
—Genesis 41:14

Day 55

Joseph's friend heard about Pharaoh's bad dream Then he remembered Joseph! He remembered when Joseph told him what his dream meant. He told Pharaoh that Joseph could explain Pharaoh's dream too. Think about how happy Joseph must have been to get out of jail!

Bad times do not last forever!

God, you are my hope!

*Then Pharaoh said to Joseph, "God has made all of this known to you.
No one is as wise and understanding as you are."*
—Genesis 41:39

Day 56

God gives us
special talents.
We should use
them to
honor him.

Joseph had a special talent from
God. He could tell people what
their dreams meant. People took
him to Pharaoh, the king in Egypt.
Pharaoh had had some bad dreams.
With God's help, Joseph told
Pharaoh what his dreams meant.
Pharaoh was grateful.

Thank you, God, for my special talents.

So Pharaoh said to Joseph, "I'm putting you in charge of the whole land of Egypt."
—Genesis 41:41

Day 57

God put Joseph in charge of all of Egypt! Joseph stored up food. Then, one day, Joseph's dream came true. His brothers had to bow down to him! Joseph realized that this was God's plan all along. Soon his brothers would understand too.

We can't always see God's plan along the way, but there will come a time when it all makes sense!

God, please show me your plan for my life!

The seven years when there was plenty of food in Egypt came to an end. Then the seven years when there wasn't enough food began. It happened just as Joseph had said it would. There wasn't enough food in any of the other lands. But in the whole land of Egypt there was food. —Genesis 41:53–54

Day 58

God knows what will happen. We should trust him.

Pharaoh's dream meant food was going to run out. But Joseph told Pharaoh what to do. God gave Joseph good ideas, and Pharaoh let Joseph save up food for the people. Then the dream came true. It was a good thing Pharaoh had trusted Joseph!

Thank you, God, for giving us good ideas!

"But God sent me ahead of you to keep some of you alive on earth. He sent me here to save your lives by an act of mighty power."
—Genesis 45:7

Day 59

God knew that the land was going to run out of food. He knew Joseph's brothers would go to Egypt to look for food. When they did, Joseph was there to give them food. God helped Joseph forgive his brothers. God made everything turn out fine.

> God knows exactly what he is doing. He is smarter than anyone!

Thank you, God, that you can use bad things for good!

Day 60

Joseph and his family were together again. God is happy when families are together.

After Joseph forgave his brothers they went to get Jacob, their father. He could not believe the great news! His favorite son was fine! And they would be living someplace safe and secure with enough to eat and drink.

Thank you, God, for fathers, sons, mothers, daughters, brothers, and sisters.

Then a new king came to power in Egypt.
Joseph didn't mean anything to him.
—Exodus 1:8

Day 61

After Joseph died, there was a new Pharaoh who did not know Joseph. The new Pharaoh was mean. He made God's people, called Israelites, work as slaves in Egypt. But God saw everything that happened to them and he had a plan.

God sees us wherever we are.

Thank you, God, that you can see me wherever I am.

After that, she couldn't hide him any longer. So she got a basket made out of the stems of tall grass. She coated the basket with tar. Then she placed the child in the basket. She put it in the tall grass that grew along the bank of the Nile River. —Exodus 2:3

Day 62

God knew his people would need a leader. He sent Moses.

Sometimes God is doing things that we can't see. When Moses was born, the slaves in Egypt had no idea that he was the one God had sent to help them. Even though Moses' mother had to send him away, God watched over him.

Thank you, God, for sending help when we need it.

Pharaoh's daughter went down to the Nile River to take a bath. Her attendants were walking along the river bank. She saw the basket in the tall grass. So she sent her female slave to get it. When she opened it, Pharaoh's daughter saw the baby. He was crying. She felt sorry for him. "This is one of the Hebrew babies," she said. —Exodus 2:5–6

Day 63

Moses' mother loved him very much. When she heard that soldiers would kill boy babies, she wanted to save Moses. She put Moses in a basket in the river. How wonderful that Pharaoh's daughter found Moses. She wanted to take care of baby Moses.

Our lives are in God's hands.

God, you know exactly what we need to do.

When the child grew older, she took him to Pharaoh's daughter.
And he became her son. She named him Moses. She said,
"I pulled him out of the water."
—Exodus 2:10

Day 64

Moses had no idea what big plans God had for him!

Moses' parents were slaves. But God worked it out so that Moses was raised by Pharaoh's daughter. He grew up in the palace! Moses saw how badly God's people were treated. He did not know that one day God would use him to rescue the people.

Thank you, God, that you will use me someday to help others.

Some shepherds came along and chased the girls away. But Moses got up and helped them. Then he gave water to their flock.
—Exodus 2:17

Day 65

God always has a plan. He makes sure we learn what we need so that we are ready for his plans. God got Moses ready for his big job too. God wanted Moses to learn about caring for many things. He wanted him to learn how to live in the desert and how to take care of himself and others.

God helps prepare us for the future.

God, teach me everything I need to be a child of God.

*"So now, go. I am sending you to Pharaoh. I want
you to bring the Israelites out of Egypt. They are my people.
—Exodus 3:10*

Day 66

God chose Moses
to rescue the
Israelites from
Egypt. He spoke
to Moses in a very
unexpected way!

Moses lived in the desert for a very long time. He took care of sheep. One day, God called to Moses from a burning bush! The bush was on fire but did not burn up. God told Moses that Moses needed to go help God's people. Moses was shocked!

Thank you, God, for your surprises!

The LORD said to him, "Who makes human beings able to talk? Who makes them unable to hear or speak? Who makes them able to see? Who makes them blind? It is I, the LORD. Now go. I will help you speak. I will teach you what to say." —Exodus 4:11–12

Day 67

God spoke to Moses. God asked him to do a big job. God believed Moses could do it! Moses was nervous. He tried to get out of the big job. But God gave Moses courage.

> God gives us strength and courage. He can help us do anything.

Thank you, God, for your strength.

So Moses got his wife and sons. He put them on a donkey. Together they started back to Egypt. And he took the walking stick in his hand. It was the stick God would use in a powerful way.
—Exodus 4:20

Day 68

Sometimes it is scary to go to where God sends us, But God will help us be brave like Moses.

Moses gathered his family and his brother together. They traveled to Egypt. They were going to see Pharaoh. God gave Moses the confidence and help he needed. Moses was still nervous, but he knew God was there with him.

God, thank you for being my guide.

Day 69

Moses and his brother Aaron went to Pharaoh. God wanted them to tell Pharaoh to let God's people leave Egypt. They told Pharaoh exactly what God wanted them to say. But Pharaoh said he would not let God's people go.

Even with God's help, sometimes things seem to get worse before they get better.

God, give me courage to keep trying.

75

So Aaron reached his hand out over the waters of Egypt.
The frogs came up and covered the land.
—Exodus 8:6

Day 70

Some people will
not obey God
no matter
what God does.

God's messages are always important. But some people, like Pharaoh, are not ready to listen. Moses asked Pharaoh to let God's people leave Egypt. Pharaoh said no. So God had a plan to show Pharaoh he was serious.

God, help me to take your word seriously.

*Then the L*ORD* said to Moses, "Go to Pharaoh. Tell him, 'The L*ORD* says, "Let my people go. Then they will be able to worship me. If you refuse to let them go, I will send a plague of frogs on your whole country."'"*
—Exodus 8:1–2

Day 71

God wanted Pharaoh to know something. He wanted Pharaoh to let the Israelites leave. So to make sure Pharaoh got the message, God used miracles called plagues to show that he was serious.

> God sent signs to show Pharaoh, the Egyptians, and the Israelites that he was serious about rescuing his people.

God, you are wise. Help me see the wisdom in everything you do.

During the night, Pharaoh sent for Moses and Aaron. He said to them, "Get out of here! You and the Israelites, leave my people! Go. Worship the LORD, just as you have asked."
—Exodus 12:31

Day 72

God's plans always work!

Moses told Pharaoh what the last plague would be. But Pharaoh did not care until his own son was gone. Finally, Pharaoh yelled, "Get out!" Then Moses led God's people out of Egypt. God knew all along that his plan would work.

God, you are powerful and use that power only for good.

The L<small>ORD</small> kept watch that night to bring them out of Egypt ...
—Exodus 12:42

Day 73

With God's help, God's people left Egypt. God guided Moses and the people every step of the way. He knew where they were going. He planned for them to be happy and free.

Just like God guided Moses and the Israelites out of Egypt, he leads us to our freedom too!

God, you know where I need to be.
You show me the ways.

By day the LORD went ahead of them in a pillar of cloud. It guided them on their way. At night he led them with a pillar of fire. It gave them light. So they could travel by day or at night.
—Exodus 13:21

Day 74

Even as God's people, we will face many challenges.

Pharaoh let God's people go, but then he changed his mind. He wanted Moses to bring the people back. Pharaoh chased God's people. They reached the Red Sea. The people were trapped!

God, I trust you to help me find my way.

"Hold out your walking stick. Reach out your hand over the Red Sea to divide the water. Then the people can go through the sea on dry ground."
—Exodus 14:16

Day 75

God's people were trapped at the Red Sea. They had nowhere to go. But that didn't stop God! He did something no one had ever done before. He parted the Red Sea! He helped Moses get the people across the sea to safety.

No matter how big the challenge, God has an answer for it!

God, you are so amazing!

*The Egyptians chased them. All Pharaoh's horses and chariots
and horsemen followed them into the sea.*
—Exodus 14:23

Day 76

Sometimes God's enemies get really mad! But God will always take care of us.

God's people were leaving Egypt! God did not want anything to ruin that. So when the Egyptians started following his people, God took care of the problem. God parted the Red Sea to help his people escape. He let the sea go back to normal to stop the Egyptians.

Thank you for your protection, God.

In the desert the whole community told Moses and
Aaron they weren't happy with them.
—Exodus 16:2

Day 77

The Israelites escaped Egypt! God had helped them get away. But even though they were free, the people were not happy. They complained about many things to Moses and Aaron. Life was not easy in the desert.

Sometimes we forget that God has done a miracle for us.

God, help me remember that all good things come from you.

The people of Israel saw the flakes. They asked each other, "What's that?" They didn't know what it was. Moses said to them, "It's the bread the LORD has given you to eat."
—Exodus 16:15

Day 78

God does not promise that every day will be easy, but he loves us and will always help us.

God led his people into the desert. They were free, but they ran out of food. They were hungry! Then God showed his people how much he loved them. He sent bread down from heaven. It was called manna. No one had ever seen it before.

God, thank you for making sure my family has what we need to live.

"I will stand there in front of you by the rock at mount Horeb. Hit the rock. Then water will come out of it for the people to drink." So Moses hit the rock while the elders of Israel watched.
—Exodus 17:6

Day 79

It was not easy for God's people to live in the desert. God supplied manna to eat, but then the people got thirsty. There was no water anywhere in sight. Did that stop God? Of course not! God made water flow out of a rock!

God wants us to trust him all the time. Sometimes it is hard for us to trust God.

God, I promise to believe that you will take care of me.

So Moses went down to the people and told them.
—Exodus 19:25

Day 80

God knows we need some rules to follow. Rules help us behave. Rules help us remember what is good and bad.

God led his people to a big mountain. He called Moses to go up to the top of the mountain. When Moses got there, God gave him ten special rules for the Israelites. God wrote them down on tablets of stone.

God, I will follow your rules.
I will follow my parents' rules too.

Day 81

God knew what was best for the Israelites. He gave Moses ten special rules for his people to live by. They were written on stone tablets in God's own handwriting! God knows what is best for us too. God still wants us to follow his Ten Commandments today.

> **God gave the Israelites the Ten Commandments. The Ten Commandments are for us too.**

1. GOD IS THE ONLY TRUE GOD.

2. NEVER MAKE IDOLS.

3. NEVER MISUSE THE LORD'S NAME.

4. REST ON THE SABBATH DAY. KEEP IT HOLY.

5. HONOR YOUR FATHER AND YOUR MOTHER.

6. DO NOT MURDER

7. HUSBANDS AND WIVES MUST NOT COMMIT ADULTERY.

8. DO NOT STEAL.

9. DO NOT TELL LIES.

10. NEVER WANT WHAT BELONGS TO OTHERS.

God, sometimes rules are hard to follow, but I will try hard to follow yours.

"Have them make a sacred tent for me. I will live among them."
—Exodus 25:8

Day 82

God wants to live with his people. God wants his people to worship him.

The Israelites traveled many years in the desert. God was always with them. The people needed a place to worship God. So God gave them directions on how to build a special tent. The tent was called a tabernacle. It was a very special place for God's people.

I will worship you, God.

So the cloud of the LORD was above the holy tent during the day. Fire was in the cloud at night. All the Israelites could see the cloud during all of their travels.
—Exodus 40:38

Day 83

After forty years in the desert, Moses and the Israelites were finally there! It was the Promised Land! It was beautiful. There was a lot of food and water. There was plenty for everyone. It was just like God had told Moses.

> Finally, God's people reached the Promised Land! God always keeps his promises.

God, you brought your people to the Promised Land. My Promised Land is heaven. You are guiding me there!

*"Here is what I am commanding you to do. Be strong and brave. Do not be afraid. Do not lose hope. I am the L*ORD *your God. I will be with you everywhere you go."*
—*Joshua 1:9*

Day 84

God wants us to be strong and brave. He promises to be with us and to help us.

After Moses died, God picked Joshua to be the new person in charge. God told Joshua to be strong and brave. God wanted him to go to the city of Jericho and take over. Joshua couldn't do it on his own, but God promised to help Joshua.

God, help me to be strong and brave like Joshua.

The woman had hidden the two men. ... She said to them ..."The LORD your God is the God who rules over heaven above and on the earth below."
—Joshua 2:4,9,11

Day 85

God wanted his people to take over the city of Jericho. Joshua sent spies to check out the city. But the king of Jericho found out. He sent soldiers to arrest the spies. But God protected them. He provided a woman to hide them on her roof.

God give us people to help us when we are doing his will.

God, people everywhere know how good you are.

Rahab went up on the roof before the spies settled down for the night. She said to them, "I know that the LORD has given you this land. We are very much afraid of you. Everyone who lives in this country is weak with fear because of you." —Joshua 2:8–9

Day 86

Sometimes our enemies are more afraid of us!

Joshua's spies were hiding from the soldiers. They were afraid. But Rahab told them the people of Jericho were more afraid. They had heard about how God dried up the Red Sea and led his people out of Egypt. They were scared of God and his people.

God, you never forget those that love you.

"March around the city once with all of your fighting men. In fact, do it for six days. Have seven priests get trumpets made out of rams' horns. They must carry them in front of the ark. On the seventh day, march around the city seven times. Tell the priests blow the trumpets as you march." —Joshua 6:3–4

Day 87

The city of Jericho had big walls around it. God gave Joshua a plan for taking over the city. The plan made no sense! But Joshua and the people followed God's instructions exactly. It all worked. Jericho's walls fell down.

God's plans don't always make sense, but they always work if we follow his directions.

God, you know how to work things out perfectly!

"Now then, please give me your word. Promise me in the name of the LORD that you will be kind to my family. I've been kind to you. Promise me that you will spare the lives of my father and mother. Spare my brothers and sisters. Also spare everyone in their families. Promise that you won't put any of us to death. —Joshua 2:12–13

Day 88

God rewards those who believe.

Rahab was not one of God's people, but she believed in God anyway. She was kind to the spies, so they promised to help her too. When God's people took over the city of Jericho, they kept Rahab and her family safe.

Thank you, God, for rewarding those who believe in you.

... The Israelites went up to her there. They came to have her decide cases for them. She settled matters between them.
—Judges 4:5

Day 89

The Israelites lived in the Promised Land for a long time. Sometimes they forgot about God. But he never forgot his people! He sent them special leaders called judges. God sent a judge named Deborah to help his people.

God never forgets his people. He watches over them like a father.

God, thank you for never forgetting us.

*Then Deborah said to Barak, "Go! Today the L*ORD *will hand Sisera over to you. Hasn't the L*ORD *gone ahead of you?" So Barak went down Mount Tabor. His 10,000 men followed him.*
—Judges 4:14

Day 90

God makes us brave when we need to be. Then we can help others.

Deborah was a leader of God's people. She was smart and brave. She helped the Israelites follow God's instructions. God wanted his army to fight a battle. They asked Deborah to come along. She helped them win the battle!

God, I will be brave and strong when you need me to be.

*"Pardon me, sir," Gideon replied, "but how can I possibly save
Israel? My family group is the weakest in the tribe of Manasseh.
And I'm the least important member of my family."*
—Judges 6:15

Day 91

God wanted Gideon to help
his people. So God sent an angel
to talk to Gideon. The angel
called Gideon a mighty warrior.
Gideon did not feel like a mighty
warrior! He didn't think he was
good enough to help. But God
knew he was!

**God does not
see us the
way we
see ourselves.**

God, please help me to see myself the way you see me.

Gideon replied, "If you are pleased with me, give me a special sign. Then I'll know that it's really you talking to me."
—Judges 6:17

Day 92

God understands if we need him to repeat his message. He knows our heart.

God told Gideon he wanted to use Gideon to save his people from their enemies. Gideon believed in God, but he was still nervous. He wanted to be extra sure. So Gideon asked God to give him a special sign.

Open my heart, God.

The LORD said to Gideon, "I want to hand Midian over to you. But you have too many men for me to do that. Then Israel might brag. 'My own strength has saved me.'"
—Judges 7:2

Day 93

Over 30,000 men wanted to join Gideon's army. But God told Gideon that was too many men. God had Gideon go to battle with only 300 men. And they won! God wanted to be sure his people knew it was God who saved them.

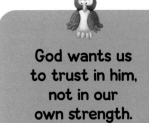

God wants us to trust in him, not in our own strength.

God, you are amazing! You are so strong!

Later, the woman had a baby boy. She named him Samson. As he grew up, the LORD blessed him. The Spirit of the LORD began to work in his life.
—Judges 13:24–25

Day 94

Some people are strong on the outside but true strength is on the inside.

Samson's mother raised her son to believe in God from the time he was born. That gave Samson strong faith plus the strength of God's love. Samson was blessed with great strength in his body. But the strength inside him was much more important!

Give me strength, dear God.

Then the Spirit of the Lord came powerfully on Samson.
—Judges 14:6

Day 95

God's people were in trouble again. So God gave a man named Samson great strength. Samson was much stronger than a normal man. Samson used his strength to keep God's people safe from the Philistines.

God sometimes gives his people special powers.

God, I want my faith to be as strong as Samson's!

Then he prayed to the LORD. Samson said, "LORD and King, show me that you still have concern for me. Please, God, make me strong just one more time. Let me pay the Philistines back for what they did to my two eyes. Let me do it with only one blow." —Judges 16:28

Day 96

Sometimes even heroes can make bad choices.

Samson was very strong. But then he made a bad choice. He did something God did not want him to do. He lost his great strength. But he did not lose God's love. He asked God to make him strong one last time, and God did it.

God, please help me make good choices.

Naomi realized that Ruth had made up her mind to go with her. So she stopped trying to make her go back.
—Ruth 1:18

Day 97

Naomi and Ruth loved each other. They would stay together no matter what. They became a good team. Life is more fun and easier when we are not alone. God gives us special friends who are always willing to help us. We should help them too.

Two are better than one. Two can share each other's burdens.

I thank you, Lord, for friends who share my burdens.

But Ruth replied, "Don't try to make me leave you and go back. Where you go I'll go. Where you stay I'll stay. Your people will be my people. Your God will be my God."
—Ruth 1:16

Day 98

God puts special, loving people into our lives.

Naomi was one of God's people. Ruth and Naomi loved each other very much. When Naomi wanted to move back to Israel, Ruth decided to go with her. Ruth said she would go wherever Naomi went and that Naomi's God would be her God.

God, thank you for my friends and family.

When Ruth heard that, she bowed down with her face
to the ground. She asked, "Why are you being so kind to me?
In fact, why are you even noticing me? I'm from another country."
—Ruth 2:10

Day 99

Ruth gave up everything when she went to Israel with Naomi. Ruth had to work in the fields to find food to eat. But God was good! The man who owned the field saw Ruth and married her. He liked how she took care of Naomi.

Being a good friend pays off!

God, I promise to be a good friend.

She made a promise to him. She said, "LORD, you rule over all. Please see how I'm suffering! Show concern for me! Don't forget about me! Please give me a son! If you do, I'll give him back to the LORD. Then he will serve the LORD all the days of his life. He'll never use a razor on his head. He'll never cut his hair." —1 Samuel 1:11

Day 100

When we really want something, it is good to ask the Lord!

Hannah and her husband wanted to have a baby. Hannah prayed and prayed to God, "Please God, send us a baby boy. If you do, I promise he will love and serve you all the days of his life." God answered her prayer!

Thank you, God, that I can come to you anytime I need something.

So after some time, Hannah became pregnant. She had a baby boy. She said, "I asked the LORD for him." So she named him Samuel.
—1 Samuel 1:20

Day 101

God heard Hannah's prayers and he saw her tears. He knew how much she wanted a baby boy. Guess what! God answered Hannah's prayers! He gave her a baby boy. She was so happy! She named him Samuel.

God answers our prayers. He knows what we need.

Thank you, Lord, for answered prayers!

"I prayed for this child. The LORD has given me what I asked him for. So now I'm giving him to the LORD. As long as he lives he'll be given to the LORD." And there Eli worshiped the LORD.
—1 Samuel 1:27–28

Day 102

God wants us all to love and serve him.

Hannah promised God that if he gave her a boy, the boy would serve God all his life. Hannah kept her promise to God. When Samuel was a little boy, she took him to see Eli, the priest. Eli lived at the temple. Eli would teach Samuel all about God.

Lord, I want to love and serve you too!

So Eli told Samuel, "Go and lie down. If someone calls out to you again, say, 'Speak, L<small>ORD</small>. I'm listening.'" So Samuel went and lay down in his place.
—1 Samuel 3:9

Day 103

One night, Samuel was sleeping. He heard someone call out, "Samuel!" Samuel asked Eli why he had called him. Eli told him to go back to bed and listen again. Eli knew it might be God talking to Samuel. Sure enough, it was!

God calls us. He wants us to listen closely.

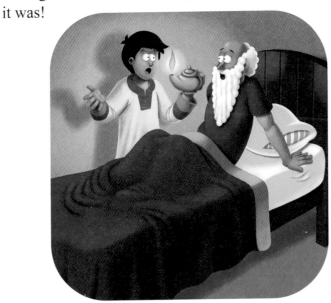

Lord, I promise to listen to you.

*The LORD came and stood there. He called out, just as he
had done the other times. He said, "Samuel! Samuel!"
Then Samuel replied, "Speak, I'm listening."*
—1 Samuel 3:10

Day 104

Sometimes God
has a very
important job
for us to do.
We need to
be ready.

God called out to Samuel in the
middle of the night! Samuel said,
"Yes, Lord. I am listening." God had
a special message for his people. It
was going to be Samuel's job to tell
the people about God.

God, whatever you need me to do, I will do it!

Samuel wasn't pleased when they said,
*"Give us a king to lead us." So he prayed to the L*ORD.
—1 Samuel 8:6

Day 105

God's people wanted a king to rule them. Samuel was a good leader so he talked to God about it. God said it was a bad idea. Samuel warned the people. But they didn't listen. They thought they knew better than God. They were wrong.

Good leaders will ask God what is best for the people.

You are the best leader, God.

They said to him, "You are old. Your sons don't live as you do. So appoint a king to lead us. We want a king just like the kings all of the other nations have."
—1 Samuel 8:5

Day 106

God always knows what is best. But God lets his people make decisions.

God's people wanted a king who would take care of them. God did not want that. He wanted to be their King. God gave the people a warning, but they did not change their minds. So God gave the Israelites a king.

God, thank you for helping me make good choices.

When Samuel saw a man coming toward him, the LORD spoke
to Samuel again. He said, "He is the man I told you about.
His name is Saul. He will govern my people."
—1 Samuel 9:17

Day 107

The Israelites wanted a king, even though that was not what God wanted for them. But God wants his people to be happy. So sometimes he gives us what we ask for. God sent Saul to the Israelites to be their king. The people were so happy!

Sometimes God gives us what we ask for, even if it is not for the best.

God, you are the one true King!

"You have done a foolish thing," Samuel said. "You haven't obeyed the command the LORD your God gave you. If you had, he would have made your kingdom secure over Israel for all time to come."
—1 Samuel 13:13

Day 108

God will never give up on his people. He knows when we need him the most.

Saul was a good king for many years. Then he made some bad choices. He disobeyed God. God was sorry he had made Saul king. God told Samuel it was time to look for a new king. Samuel was sad that Saul had disobeyed God.

God, I never want to make you sad!

But the LORD said to Samuel, "Do not consider how handsome or tall he is. I have not chosen him. The LORD does not look at the things people look at. People look at the outside of a person. But the LORD looks at what is in the heart." —1 Samuel 16:7

Day 109

God sent Samuel to see a man named Jesse. God told Samuel that one of Jesse's sons would be the next king for God's people. Jesse had eight sons. But it was not until Samuel saw the youngest son, David, that Samuel said, "That's the one!"

God knows that how we look is not the most important thing. God looks at our hearts.

Help me, Lord, to have a good heart.

So Samuel got the animal horn that was filled with olive oil. He anointed David in front of his brothers. From that day on, the Spirit of the LORD came powerfully on David. Samuel went back to Ramah.
—1 Samuel 16:13

Day 110

When God chooses us for a special job, he gives us the power to do it.

God told Samuel that David was God's choice to be the new king. David was a good boy. He loved God very much. Samuel told David he was going to be king someday. Samuel poured oil on David's head. God's power came on David.

God, I will be ready when you need me.

Whenever Israel's army saw Goliath, all of them ran away from him. That's because they were so afraid.
—1 Samuel 17:24

Day 111

The Israelite army was scared of Goliath. Not one man was brave enough to face the giant. Then David came into the camp. He was not afraid! Think about what might have happened if David had been afraid too! No one would have faced Goliath!

We don't have to be afraid just because everyone else is afraid.

God, help me be strong even if others are not.

Saul replied, "You aren't able to go out there and fight that Philistine. You are too young. He's been a warrior ever since he was a boy."
—1 Samuel 17:33

Day 112

You don't have to be a big person to have confidence in our great big God!

David was a young boy. But he trusted God. He knew God was always with him. David told King Saul that he was not afraid. David was ready to fight the giant Goliath. He wanted to show everyone how strong God was.

Let me be an example of big faith in a big God!

"The LORD saved me from the paw of the lion. He saved me from the paw of the bear. And he'll save me from the powerful hand of this Philistine too."
—1 Samuel 17:37a

Day 113

David heard about the giant Goliath. His brothers were too afraid to fight. But not David! David believed God was bigger and strong than any giant! God had always helped David before. David knew God would help this time too.

We have to trust God all the time, no matter how big the challenge.

God, I cannot do anything without you.

Saul said to David, "Go. And may the L<small>ORD</small> be with you."
—1 Samuel 17:37b

Day 114

God does not expect us to face giant challenges without his help.

Goliath was a giant man. His army wanted the Israelites to be their slaves. God's people were led by King Saul. But King Saul's army was too scared of Goliath to fight. How would God help his people this time?

God, help me understand I cannot do everything alone.

Then Saul dressed David in his own military clothes ...
—1 Samuel 17:38

Day 115

Saul wanted to help the young boy David. David was brave and wanted to fight Goliath. But he did not have armor. King Saul gave David his own armor! But would it work? God knows exactly what we need when we are fighting for him.

God knows what we need to wear to fight a battle for God.

Your love is what I need for protection, God.

Day 116

It doesn't matter what other people think of us. We are mighty in God!

David knew he was small. He knew he was young. But that did not matter to David. David knew that God's love made him big and strong. David knew that he was more powerful than Goliath because God was with him.

Make me mighty in your love, God.

David said to Goliath, "You are coming to fight against me with a sword, a spear and a javelin. But I'm coming against you in the name of the Lord who rules over all."
—1 Samuel 17:45

Day 117

David chose stones and a slingshot to use when he fought Goliath. But more important than those things, David had faith in God. He knew in his heart that God would take care of everything. And God did! David beat Goliath in the fight. Think about how strong you could be if you believed in God like David!

God gives us the right weapons to fight for him. Our best weapon is prayer!

God, please give me faith as strong as David's faith.

"This day the Lord will give me victory over you ...
Then the whole world will know there is a God in Israel."
—1 Samuel 17:46

Day 118

Goliath was a giant man, but David had giant faith in God. Giant faith wins!

David was very brave. He fought Goliath with just a sling and a stone. Goliath was a giant with a big sword, but David's God was even bigger! David won the battle. He saved God's people.

God, I want giant faith too.

*He reached into his bag. He took out a stone. He put it in his
sling. He slung it at Goliath. The stone hit him on the forehead
and sank into it. He fell to the ground on his face.*
—1 Samuel 17:49

Day 119

David stepped up to Goliath.
He took out his small weapons.
God gave him the courage and
strength to aim and throw the stone
at Goliath. With God by his side,
David knew he could do anything,
and he did! He beat Goliath. He
helped save God's people.

**God can give
us supernatural
courage.**

My courage comes from you, God.

Then the men of Israel and Judah shouted and rushed forward. They chased the Philistines to the entrance of Gath. They chased them to the gates of Ekron. Bodies of dead Philistine were scattered all along the road to Gath and Ekron. That's the road that leads to Shaaraim. —1 Samuel 17:52

Day 120

When we win a victory for God, it helps other people too!

David's victory over Goliath was a victory for God. It was a victory for God's people too. Seeing how brave David had been, the Israelite soldiers became braver. They helped beat the rest of the Philistine army. God's strength is for everyone, not just some people.

I will always be open to your help, God.

The next day an evil spirit sent by God came powerfully on Saul. Saul began to prophesy in his house. At that same time David began to play the harp, just as he usually did.
—1 Samuel 18:10

Day 121

Sometimes King Saul was grumpy. So David played his harp and sang for him. What a good help that was!

God wants me to use my talents like David used his talents.

God, help me be generous and kind with my talents.

Jonathan made a covenant with David because
he loved him just as he loved himself.
—1 Samuel 18:3

Day 122

Friends are one of God's best gifts.

King Saul used to feel sad a lot. David would come and play his harp to help the king feel better. One day, when David was helping King Saul, he met the king's son Jonathan. David and Jonathan became best friends.

God, help me show my friends how much I love them.

From that time on, Saul watched David closely.
—1 Samuel 18:9

Day 123

Everyone liked David. He was a nice man. He was brave and strong. He won lots of battles. The people said David was a better fighter than King Saul. That made King Saul upset! King Saul was jealous. He wanted to get rid of David.

God does not want us to be jealous. Being jealous breaks one of his Ten Commandments!

God, help me be myself even if other people do not like it.

But Jonathan liked David very much. So Jonathan warned him ...
—1 Samuel 19:1–2

Day 124

God wants us to love our friends and be good to them.

Jonathan's dad, King Saul, did not like Jonathan's best friend, David. Jonathan told David to go far away. He wanted his friend to stay safe. Jonathan and David were both sad when David left. But Jonathan was happy he helped his friend.

God, if my friend needs me, I will help!

After Saul and Jonathan died, David asked the LORD for advice.
—2 Samuel 2:1

Day 125

David had to hide from Saul for a long time. Then one day he heard that King Saul was dead. David knew it was time for him to be king. God had chosen him to lead God's people. But David knew he would need God's help.

> When it is time to do a big job, we need to ask God for help.

God, as long as I have your help,
I will be ready to do anything!

Then the men of Judah came to Hebron. There they
anointed David to be king over the people of Judah.
—2 Samuel 2:4

Day 126

Nations need good,
faithful leaders.
God knows what
is in a good
leader's heart.

God's people needed a good, strong leader who loved God. God had prepared David to be a good king. The people saw that he was a smart and brave man. But most importantly they knew that David loved God. David would be a good leader for God's people.

**Please bless our world leaders and give
them hearts for you, God.**

*Lᴏʀᴅ, in the morning you hear my voice. In the morning
I pray to you. I wait for you in hope.*
—Psalm 5:3

Day 127

To get to know God, we have to talk with him. That's why praying is so important! We can pray out loud or we can talk to him quietly in our heads and hearts. God can hear us no matter what! And when we listen very closely, God answers us!

God wants his people to spend time alone with him. He wants us to listen to what he has to say.

Please hear my prayers!

133

The Lord is my shepherd. He gives me everything I need.
—Psalm 23:1

Day 128

The Lord is our shepherd. He watches over our lives.

David thought of God as a good shepherd who was always watching over him. Like a good shepherd, God guides us in the right paths. He gives us what we need. God's love and goodness are with us every day, forever.

Thank you, Lord, for leading me like a good shepherd.

Even though I walk through the darkest valley,
I will not be afraid. You are with me.
—Psalm 23:4

Day 129

David wrote many songs and poems about God's goodness. They are called psalms. They tell us about God, his great love, and how he helps his people.

With God as our shepherd, we do not need to be afraid.

God, the psalms David wrote are beautiful!

Remember the wonderful things he has done.
Remember his miracles and how he judged our enemies.
—Psalm 105:5

Day 130

It is good for us to look back on the victories God has given. It is good to remember the miracles.

God does many good things for us. He wants to make us happy. He cares about us! We need to always remember the good things God has done for us in our past. David remembered the times God helped him kill a lion and a bear to save the sheep.

I am filled with joy!

"He said, 'I praise the LORD. He is the God of Israel. He has let me live to see my son sitting on my throne today as the next king.'"
—1 Kings 1:48

Day 131

David loved God with all of his heart. He was king over God's people until he was very old. David made plans for his son to build God a temple. David wanted to be sure the people never forgot about God.

God wants us to love him for our whole life long.

I love you with all of my heart, God.

Day 132

Good parents who love God will pass on their faith to their children.

One of King David's sons was named Solomon. David taught Solomon to love God very much. David wanted Solomon to be the king of Israel after him. When David died, Solomon became the new king.

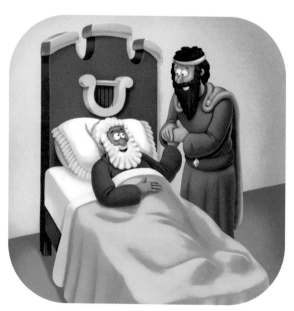

I will respect my mother and father, God.

Solomon showed his love for the LORD. He did it by
obeying the laws his father David had taught him.
—1 Kings 3:3

Day 133

Solomon became king after his
father David. Solomon wanted to
bring glory to God. He wanted to
follow God's laws. Solomon cared
about the people. Solomon used his
gifts to honor God in many ways.
That made God happy, so he blessed
Solomon.

God delights
in those who
honor him.

God, I hope I bring you happiness every day.

The LORD appeared to Solomon at Gibeon. He spoke to him in a dream during the night. God said, "Ask for anything you want me to give you."
—1 Kings 3:5

Day 134

Wisdom is more than just being smart. Wise people make godly choices.

Solomon had a dream. In the dream, God said he would give Solomon whatever he asked for! Solomon asked God to make him wise and to show him the difference between right and wrong. God was so proud of Solomon.

Lord, I want to be wise like Solomon.

"I will give it to you. I will give you a wise and understanding heart. So here is what will be true of you. There has never been anyone like you. And there never will be."
—1 Kings 3:12

Day 135

God made King Solomon very wise. Solomon made many wise decisions. He wrote wise sayings called proverbs to teach others what was right and true. People from all over the world came to hear Solomon's wisdom.

When God gives us wisdom, other people will notice!

Lord, help me to make wise decisions.

*... They saw that God had given him wisdom. They knew that
Solomon would do what was right and fair when he judged people.*
—1 Kings 3:28

Day 136

Wisdom can be
used to show
God you love him.

Think about what you could do
with wisdom like Solomon's.
Solomon used his wisdom to
honor God and help others. He
built a temple for God's people.
It was a special place for them to
worship God.

Guide me like you guided Solomon.

"But you must walk with me, just as your father David did. Your heart must be honest. It must be without blame. Do everything I command you to do. Obey my rules and laws. Then I will set up your royal throne over Israel forever. I promised your father David I would do that. I said to him, 'You will always have a son from your family line on the throne of Israel.'" —1 Kings 9:4–5

Day 137

Solomon worked hard as king. God helped Solomon do his job! God used Solomon to show the people how to follow God's ways. God knows people make mistakes, but he is with us every day.

God wants to be involved in our lives. He wants us to always obey his rules.

Lord, I want to honor you like Solomon did!

Ahab, the son of Omri, did what was evil in the sight of the LORD. He did more evil things than any of the kings who had ruled before him.
—1 Kings 16:30

Day 138

Some people worship false gods. False gods are all around us.

King Ahab was not a good king. He did not love God. He worshiped false gods. Ahab did not understand that God was the one true God and that God was the only God. Soon God's people followed Ahab's bad ways. God was not happy with Ahab.

Help me keep my eyes on you, God.

It was now three years since it had rained. A message came to Elijah from the LORD. He said, "Go. Speak to Ahab. Then I will send rain on the land."
—1 Kings 18:1

Day 139

God's love lasts forever. That is a long time! God never forgets about his people. But sometimes, God's people forget about him. Then God will send them special messengers like Elijah to remind them.

Sometimes God's own people forgot about him and his love.

Lord, please help me never to forget about you!

"... And you can be just as sure that there won't be any dew or rain on the whole land. There won't be any during the next few years. It won't come until I say so."
—1 Kings 17:1

Day 140

When God sends messages to his people, we should listen.

God's people were not thinking about him. Their new king did not love God. But God still loved his people! He wanted to get the people's attention. So he stopped the rain from coming. God wanted the people to call out to him.

Lord, help us hear when you send us a message!

So Elijah did what the Lord had told him to do. He went to the Kerith Valley. It was east of the Jordan River. He stayed there. The ravens brought him bread and meat in the morning. They also brought him bread and meat in the evening. He drank water from the brook. —1 Kings 17:5–6

Day 141

Listening to God's Word is the best way to stay strong. But God knows we sometimes need other things too. Elijah ran away from Ahab. Elijah was tired and hungry. God sent birds to bring food to Elijah! God is our source of strength, just like he was for Elijah.

When we are tired and hungry. God will take care of us.

You are my strength and hope, God

147

*"Stay there, I have directed a widow there to supply you with food."
So Elijah went to Zarephath. He came to the town gate. A widow
was there gathering sticks. He called out to her. He asked, "Would
you bring me a little water in a jar? I need a drink."* —1 Kings 17:9–10

Day 142

Sometimes God will send one of his special servants into our lives to help us.

God has special servants everywhere, all the time. When we need someone like that, God makes sure to send us a helper! One of God's special helpers from long ago was the prophet Elijah. God sent Elijah to help a poor widow who was very hungry.

Am I one of your special servants, Lord?

She went away and did what Elijah had told her to do. So Elijah had food every day. There was also food for the woman and her family. The jar of flour wasn't used up. The jug always had oil in it. That's what the LORD had said would happen. He had spoken that message through Elijah. —1 Kings 17:15–16

Day 143

Would you share your last bite of food? A poor widow shared hers with God's servant Elijah. It was so nice of her to help! Because she helped Elijah, God made sure that food for her family never ran out!

God will always help the people who love him.

Lord, teach me to be a giving person, even if it seems hard.

It was now three years since it had rained. A message came to Elijah from the LORD. He said, "Go. Speak to Ahab. Then I will send rain on the land." So Elijah went to speak to Ahab. There wasn't enough food in Samaria. The people there were very hungry. —1 Kings 18:1–2

Day 144

Sometimes God uses us to deliver messages. We must be ready and willing to help.

God has many ways of letting people know what he wants. Sometimes he uses people who love him to tell something important to someone else. People who love God should be ready to serve him. God has special people called prophets who are helpers for God.

God, I am ready and willing to help.

"I haven't made trouble for Israel," Elijah replied. "But you and your father's family have. You have turned away from the LORD's commands. You have followed the gods that are named after Baal."
—1 Kings 18:18

Day 145

Some people put their faith in false gods. They believe that stone or wood statues have more power than the one true God! Stone and wood have no power at all. Only God can love and care for us the way God does. Only God can give us everything we need.

> An idol is a false god. It cannot help anyone.

God, you are the one true God!

Obadiah went back to Ahab. He told Ahab that Elijah wanted to see him. So Ahab went to where Elijah was. When he saw Elijah, he said to him, "Is that you? You are always stirring up trouble in Israel."
—1 Kings 18:16–17

Day 146

God wants his people to praise only him!

King Ahab was a very bad king. He bowed down to Baal, a pretend god. He would not teach his people about the one true God. He would not follow God's commands. So God made a plan to prove he was the real God.

Lord, keep me away from false gods.

"Get two bulls for us. Let Baal's prophets choose one for themselves. Let them cut it into pieces. Then let them put it on the wood. But don't let them set fire to it. I'll prepare the other bull. I'll put it on the wood. But I won't set fire to it. Then you pray to your god. And I'll pray to the LORD. The god who answers by sending fire down is the one and only God." —1 Kings 18:23–24

Day 147

Elijah had great faith. His God was the only real God. Elijah decided to prove it! He challenged King Ahab and the people who believed in false gods. Elijah knew that God would support him. He knew that God never fails. He is mighty and powerful! God is always our strength and hope.

Our God is the one true God. We can have confidence in him.

I have confidence in you, God!

When it was time to offer the evening sacrifice, the prophet Elijah stepped forward. He prayed, "LORD, you are the God of Abraham, Isaac and Israel. Today let everyone know that you are God in Israel. Let them know I'm your servant." —1 Kings 18:36

Day 148

God is the one true God!

No matter what they did, King Ahab's men could not get their altar to Baal to burn. Baal was a pretend god. But when Elijah prayed to his God, fire came from heaven. Elijah's whole alter, and everything around it, burned up! It was a miracle!

Lord, you can do anything.

All of the people saw it. Then they fell down flat with their faces toward the ground. They cried out, "The LORD is the one and only God! The LORD is the one and only God!"
—1 Kings 18:39

Day 149

Think about how God's people felt when Elijah's altar burned right up! They were not confused anymore. They could see that their God was the real God! They saw God's power. He had been with them the whole time.

God understands that sometimes even his own people need proof that he still cares for them.

Lord, if I forget you, even for a minute, please send me a reminder.

Elijah left Mount Horeb. He saw Elisha, the son of Shaphat. Elisha was plowing in a field. He was driving the last of 12 pairs of oxen. Elijah went up to him. He threw his coat around him. Then Elisha left his oxen. He ran after Elijah. "Let me kiss my father and mother good-bye," he said. "Then I'll come with you." —1 Kings 19:19–20

Day 150

> God always has a plan. We don't always know God's plans for us until they happen!

When God made us, he gave us free will. That means we can make choices. But God's plans are better than our plans. God knows what is best and what should happen in our lives. He will let us know his plans when he is ready to tell us. He likes to surprise us!

I am ready when you are, God!

So Elisha left him and went back. He got his two oxen and killed them. He burned the plow to cook the meat. He gave it to the people, and they ate it. Then he started to follow Elijah. He became Elijah's servant.
—*2 Kings 19:21*

Day 151

God chose a man named Elisha to be Elijah's helper. They worked together to bring God's message to the people. God knew that Elijah was getting old and one day someone would need to take over Elijah's job.

> Even God's leaders need helpers sometimes.

Lord, is there anyone I can help?

Elijah rolled up his coat. Then he struck the water
with it. The water parted to the right and to the left. The two
of them went across the river on dry ground.
—2 Kings 2:8

Day 152

God's power is great! Even when there are very few people around to see it, his power is there.

God has lots of power. If he wanted to, he could show it off all the time, in big ways. But God does not have to show off his power. We can see his power in little things all around us, all the time. Sometimes he does big things. Sometimes we are the only ones to see it!

How great is your power and love, God!

After they had gone cross, Elijah said to Elisha, "Tell me,
what can I do for you before I am taken away from you?"
"Please give me a double share of your spirit," Elisha replied.
—2 Kings 2:9

Day 153

Elijah was old and ready to go to heaven. He asked Elisha if he wanted anything. Elisha asked for a double share of God's power. Elijah said, "Only God can give you that. But if you see me when I leave, then you will get it."

Elisha saw a chariot and fiery horses take the prophet Elijah to heaven.

I want more of your power, Lord!

Elisha replied to her, "How can I help you? Tell me. What do you have in your house?"
—2 Kings 4:2

Day 154

God loves us, and he is bigger than our problems.

A woman was in trouble. She owed a man some money. But she didn't have any, so the man wanted to take her sons away. She needed help! She went to Elisha, the man of God. He knew that God was bigger than the woman's problem.

Thank you, God, that we can always come to you for help!

The woman left him. Then she shut the door behind her and her sons.
They brought the jars to her. And she kept pouring.
—2 Kings 4:5

Day 155

A woman who owed money had only a tiny bit of oil. Elisha told her to put it into jars and sell it to make money. It wasn't enough oil, but she did not argue. The woman did what Elisha said. As soon as she poured the oil in the jars, there was lots of oil! It was a miracle!

Sometimes God does impossible things called miracles to help people!

God, you can do anything!

The woman said to her husband, "That man often comes by here. I know that he is a holy man of God. Let's make a small room for him on the roof. We'll put a bed and a table in it. We'll also put a chair and a lamp in it. Then he can stay there when he comes to visit us." —2 Kings 4:9–10

Day 156

The best friends are the ones with whom you can share your love of God.

Elisha worked hard for God. He made some good friends. One couple even set up a room just for him. They knew Elisha was a man of God. They wanted him to have a special place to stay. It is good to have friends who love God.

God, help me find good friends who love you.

He said to Gehazi, "Tell her, 'You have gone to a lot of trouble for us. Now what can we do for you? Can we speak to the king for you? Or can we speak to the commander of the army for you?'"
—2 Kings 4:13

Day 157

God gave his prophets some special skills and knowledge. The prophets could use those skills or knowledge to help people. Elisha wanted to make sure that the woman and her husband who helped him knew he was grateful. He wanted them to feel God's love too.

It is good to be kind to God's helpers.

I can feel your love, God.

"You will hold a son in your arms," Elisha said.
"It will be about this time next year."
—2 Kings 4:16

Day 158

God rewards people who help his servants.

Elisha wanted to do something special for the woman who helped him. She had no children and her husband was old. Elisah said, "You will have a son." She didn't believe it. But God gave her a baby boy. It was a miracle!

I want to be your servant, O Lord.

Naaman was an army commander of the king of Aram. He was very important to his master and was highly respected. That's because the Lord had helped him win the battle over Aram's enemies. He was a brave soldier. But he had a skin disease. —2 Kings 5:1

Day 159

No matter how big or scary, God can help us with our problems. That is what we believe! That is what Naaman needed to believe too. Naaman had a bad skin disease. He couldn't cure it. Just when his problem seemed too hard, God stepped in to help him!

> Sometimes our problems seem too big. We need help to solve them.

I know you will always help me, God!

The young girl spoke to the woman she was serving. She said, "I wish my master would go and see the prophet who is in Samaria. He would heal my master of his skin disease."
—2 Kings 5:3

Day 160

We should tell people that God can help them.

Naaman was a brave man. But Naaman had a very bad skin disease. His wife's servant girl believed in God. The servant told Naaman to go to Israel and see God's messenger, Elisha. She knew God could heal Naaman.

Help me tell other people about you, Lord.

"... Tell the man to come to me.
Then he will know there is a prophet in Israel."
—2 Kings 5:8

Day 161

Naaman went to Elisha for help. Elisha told Naaman to wash in the Jordan River seven times. Naaman was mad at first. He didn't believe Elisha. But when he washed, it worked! Naaman was healed. God healed Naaman even though he didn't believe in God.

God is amazing!

Thank you, God, for helping people who don't even know you.

Naaman and all of his attendants went back to the man of God. Naaman stood in front of Elisha. Naaman said, "Now I know that there is no God anywhere in the whole world except in Israel. So please accept a gift from me."—2 Kings 5:15

Day 162

God wants people from everywhere to know he is the one true God.

There can only be one, true God. Naaman found out that God is the One! God's power and love for Naaman showed when God cured Naaman's skin disease. Naaman was so joyful. He wanted everyone to know about God! He wanted to show his love back.

How can I show you I love you, God?

Josiah did what was right in the eyes of the LORD. He lived the way King David had lived. He didn't turn away from it to the right or the left.
—2 Kings 22:2

Day 163

Josiah was a little boy. He loved God very much. He became king when he was only eight years old. Can you imagine being king when you are still a child! King Josiah did many good things. He was a good example to the people.

> **It does not matter how old you are, God can use you.**

Thank you, God, that you use children to do big things!

"Have them put all of the money in the care of certain men. These men have been put in charge of the work on the LORD's temple. Have them pay the workers who repair it. Have them pay the builders and those who work with wood. Have them pay those who lay the stones. Also have them buy lumber and blocks of stone to repair the temple."—2 Kings 22:5–6

Day 164

God wants his people to care about the place where they worship.

A temple is a place of worship. It is a special place for people to go and be near God. God wants us to care for our places of worship. He wants us to give time and money to keep them repaired. God wants his house to feel like a special home for people on earth.

Thank you for welcoming me into your home!

The king stood next to his pillar. He agreed to the terms of the covenant in front of the LORD. The king promised to serve the LORD and obey his commands, directions and rules ...
—2 King 23:3

Day 165

A treasure is something special that we care for. A treasure is something we tell people about. King Josiah's men found a scroll hidden in the temple wall. It was the Book of God's Law! It was the best treasure they could have found! It was the Word of God!

The Word of God is the greatest treasure! It is a treasure to be shared.

Your Word is a treasure, God.

... He promised to obey them with all his heart and with all his soul. So he agreed to the terms of the covenant written down in that book. Then all the people committed themselves to the covenant as well.
—2 Kings 23:3

Day 166

We should live according to God's law.

King Josiah decided to fix up the temple. He wanted people to worship God there. When the temple was being fixed up, a special scroll was found. It was God's Laws! King Josiah read the scrolls to the people. They promised to follow God.

I promise to follow you too, Lord.

There was no king like Josiah either before him or after him. None of them turned to the LORD as he did. He obeyed the LORD with all his heart and with all his soul He obeyed him with all his strength. He did everything the Law of Moses required. —2 King 23:25

Day 167

King Josiah was a good leader. His people followed his example. The people loved God and worshiped him. They promised to obey God's laws, just like King Josiah did. God was happy with King Josiah and the people for promising to obey him!

God loves it when the leader and all the people of the nation obey God's laws.

God, bless our nations and leaders everywhere.

Day 168

When we are beautiful on the inside, it shows on the outside.

Esther was beautiful on the outside, but she was also very nice. She cared about her family, and she cared about the Jewish people. Esther did not know it, but her beauty would be noticed by important people! One day this beauty would help her be chosen as queen!

God, help me to be a beautiful person on the inside.

Day 169

The king of Persia was looking for new queen. Esther was a beautiful Jewish woman. She was sent to the palace with many other women. But the king chose her to be queen! It would be a big job, but Esther would do it.

God has plans that we do not know anything about.

I have faith in your plans for me, Lord.

The king liked Esther more than he liked any of the other women. She pleased him more than any of the other virgins. So he put a royal crown on her head. He made her queen in Vashti's place.
—Esther 2:17

Day 170

> When God has a plan, God makes his people shine above others.

The king of Persia wanted a new queen. The king talked with many women. They were all beautiful. But when the king met Esther, he knew she was very special! He saw her beauty. He thought, "She is just the right one to be my queen!"

Let me be a help to you, God.

Then the king gave a feast to honor Esther. All his nobles and officials were invited. He announced a holiday all throughout the territories he ruled over. He freely gave many gifts in keeping with his royal wealth.
—Esther 2:18

Day 171

The king was happy that Esther was his new queen! He threw a big party. He gave people gifts. God was glad that Esther became queen too. It was his idea! He had a plan, and he wanted Esther's help. God's people were also happy. Now they had a queen that loved God too!

When God's people become leaders like he wants, God is happy! God's people are happy too!

I want to make you happy, God.

All of the royal officials at the palace gate got down on their knees. They gave honor to Haman. That's because the king had commanded them to do it. But Mordecai refused to get down on his knees. He wouldn't give Haman any honor at all. —Esther 3:2

Day 172

If you love God, you will bow down only to him.

Haman was one of the king's helpers. All the royal officials at the king's gate knelt down and paid honor to Haman. That was the rule of the king. But Esther's cousin Mordecai would not kneel down or pay honor to Haman. Mordecai would only bow down to God.

Help me stay as strong and faithful as Mordecai, God.

All the Jews were very sad. They didn't eat anything. They wept and cried. Many of them put on the rough clothing people wear when they're sad. They were lying down in ashes. They did all of those things in every territory where the king's order and law had been sent. —Esther 4:3

Day 173

Haman was the king's helper. He was not a good man. He did not love God. He hated the Jewish people. But the Jewish people were God's people! Haman made a plan to kill them all. He lied to the king and tricked him into signing a bad law that would hurt God's people.

God has enemies, so God's people have enemies too.

Protect us, God, from our enemies.

"What if you don't say anything at this time? Then help for the Jews will come from another place. But you and your family will die. Who knows? It's possible that you became queen for a time just like this."
—Esther 4:14

Day 174

God makes us brave when we need to be.

Esther and the Jewish people were in trouble. They prayed and prayed. Esther's cousin Mordecai said maybe this was why God had made her queen. It was part of God's plan! Esther had to be brave and go see the king.

When I have something hard to do, I know you are with me, O Lord.

"Go. Gather together all of the Jews who are in Susa. And fast for my benefit. Don't eat or drink anything for three days. Don't do it night or day. I and my attendants will fast just as you do. Then I'll go to the king. I'll do it even though it's against the law. And if I have to die, I'll die." —Esther 4:16

Day 175

When Esther heard that her people were in trouble, she knew she had to do something. She prayed to God for three days. She asked Mordecai and all God's people to do the same. Esther knew she might be in danger. But helping God's people was more important.

When there is a really serious situation, pray hard!

Help me be ready to serve you, God.

He saw Queen Esther standing in the courtyard. He was pleased with her. So he reached out toward her the gold scepter that was in his hand. Then Esther approached him. She touched the top of the scepter.
—Esther 5:2

Day 176

God helped Esther think of a good plan. God's plans work.

There was a rule that said people could not see the king any time they wanted. They would be put to death unless the king extended his gold rod. Esther was afraid. But she went anyway! God gave her a plan. God gave her courage. The king was happy to see Esther. He extended his gold scepter to her!

Help me trust in your plans. God

King Xerxes asked Queen Esther, "Who is the man who has dared to do such a thing? And where is he?"
—Esther 7:5

Day 177

Esther told the king about the problem. The Jewish people, including Esther, were in danger! The king was very angry. He did not want Esther and her people to be killed! So the king had Haman arrested. He punished Haman. The king helped to stop Haman's evil plan.

God caused the enemy of his people to be arrested—just in time!

God, thank you for stepping in to protect your people!

The king took his ring off. It had his royal mark on it. He had taken it back from Haman. Now he gave it to Mordecai. And Esther put Mordecai in charge of everything Haman had owned.
—Esther 8:2

Day 178

God rewards people who are faithful to him.

The king was glad that he listened to Esther. Esther told the king that Mordecai was her cousin and that he had helped her. So the king gave Haman's job to Mordecai. The king knew that Mordecai was a good man. Mordecai would be a good helper to the king.

Help me be faithful like Esther, God.

"Now write another order in my name. Do it for the benefit of the Jews. Do what seems best to you. Stamp the order with my royal mark. Nothing that is written in my name and stamped with my mark can ever be changed." —Esther 8:8

Day 179

The king told Esther and Mordecai that they could do whatever they wanted to be sure the Jewish people were safe. So they made a new law saying God's people could fight back against their enemies. God's people fought back and all their enemies were destroyed.

God saved the Jewish people from their enemies who wanted to kill them!

Thank you, God, for saving the Jewish people!

The Jews were filled with joy and happiness. They were very glad because now they were being honored.
—Esther 8:16

Day 180

God protects his people. He will always love us.

God used Esther to save the Jewish people! He planned for her to be queen at just the right time. She was there to stop Haman's evil plan. God loves his people. He watches over them.

You never forget your people, Lord.

They celebrated and enjoyed good food. They were glad and full of joy. That was true everywhere the king's order came. It was true in every territory and every city.
—Esther 8:17

Day 181

God's plan worked. With the help of Esther, Mordecai, and the king, God took care of his people just like he planned! God's people were saved. Their enemies were destroyed. God cares for and protects his people. That is a great reason to celebrate!

God stops the plans of his enemies! That is a reason for his people to celebrate his love.

I celebrate your love, God!

Day 182

Daniel grew up in a foreign country, far away from home. But God was with him. He is always with us too.

Daniel loved God. He lived in the land of Judah. The king of Babylon attacked Judah. He took Daniel back to his country to live. Daniel was very smart, so he was chosen to be a helper to the king. Even in a foreign country, God was still with Daniel!

Thank you, God, that wherever I am, you are there!

He asked them for advice in matters that required wisdom and understanding. The king always found their answers to be the best. Other men in his kingdom claimed to get knowledge by using magic.
—Daniel 1:20

Day 183

Daniel studied for three years. He worked hard to learn everything he could. Then he served the king. Daniel did a great job! God guided Daniel as he helped the king. God gave Daniel wisdom. Daniel could answer the king's questions better than the king's own people.

The king was impressed with Daniel. God blessed Daniel with special wisdom.

Help me to use my knowledge to give you glory, God.

Then Nebuchadnezzar was very angry with Shadrach, Meshach and Abednego. The look on his face changed. And he ordered that the furnace be heated seven times hotter than usual.
—Daniel 3:19

Day 184

We are not to bow down to any other gods but the one true God.

Shadrach, Meshach, and Abednego knew their God was the one true God. They knew about God's rule that they should only worship him. So they refused to bow down to another god. But that made the king of Babylon very mad.

Give me faith to follow your rules, Lord.

Then King Nebuchadnezzar leaped to his feet. He was so amazed he asked his advisers, "Didn't we tie up three men? Didn't we throw three men into the fire?" They replied, "Yes, we did, Your Majesty." The king said, "Look! I see four men walking around in the fire. They aren't tied up. And the fire hasn't even harmed them. The fourth man looks like a son of the gods.—Daniel 3:24–25

Day 185

Shadrach, Meshach, and Abednego were in trouble with the king. He made a big furnace very hot and threw them into the fire! But God takes care of his followers. The three men were not even burned! God sent his angel to protect them.

God protects the faithful.

We do not need to be scared, Lord.

Then Nebuchadnezzar said, "May the God of Shadrach, Meshach and Abednego be praised! He has sent his angel and saved his servants. They trusted in him. They refused to obey my command. They were willing to give up their lives. They would rather die than serve or worship any god except their own God. —Daniel 3:28

Day 186

God shows people who don't know him signs so that they can believe too.

The king was amazed that Shadrach, Meshach, and Abednego were fine. The fire had not hurt them. The king praised their God! He said everyone should know about how great God really is!

I know you will save me, God.

Finally these men said, "We want to bring charges against this man Daniel. But it's almost impossible for us to come up with a reason to do it. If we find a reason, it will have to be in connection with the law of his God."
—Daniel 6:5

Day 187

Daniel was King Darius' best helper. But the other helpers did not like Daniel. They thought of a way to hurt Daniel. Daniel loved God. So the other helpers got the king to make a law that said people could pray only to the king.

Daniel was a faithful man who loved to pray to God.

Lord, I promise to pray to you every day.

Daniel found out that the king had signed the order. In spite of that, he did just as he had always done before. He went home to his upstairs room. Its windows opened toward Jerusalem. He went to his room three times a day to pray. He got down on his knees and gave thanks to his God. —Daniel 6:10

Day 188

Daniel prayed to God every single day at least three times a day. We should talk with God every day!

The king was talked into making a new law. No one could pray to anyone except him or they would be thrown into the lions' den. Daniel would never follow that rule! He loved God. He wanted to pray to him every day. He wanted to praise God every day. Daniel did not care about the new law.

God, I want to praise and thank you every day!

So they went to the king. They spoke to him about his royal order. They said, "Your Majesty, didn't you sign an official order? It said that for the next 30 days your people could pray only to you. They could not pray to anyone else, whether god or human being. If they did, they would be thrown into the lions' den." The king answered, "The order must still be obeyed. It's what the law of the Medes and Persians requires. So it can't be changed."—Daniel 6:12

Day 189

Daniel did not stop praying to God. So some men arrested him. They brought Daniel to the king. The king was stuck! The king loved Daniel, but he had to follow his rule. Daniel's love of God got Daniel into trouble. But Daniel was brave. He believed that God would help him.

> **Daniel was arrested for obeying God's laws. Obeying God should be important no matter what the consequences.**

God, help me follow your rules even if it gets hard.

Day 190

Even when
things go wrong,
God has not
forgotten us.

Daniel was thrown into the lions'
den. This was not good news. But God
knew what was happening to Daniel.
God knew how strong Daniel's faith
was. And Daniel knew how strong
God was! Daniel trusted God. He
knew what was happening was part
of God's plan.

I can count on your love, God!

When he got near it, he called out to Daniel. His voice was filled with great concern. He said, "Daniel! You serve the living God. You always serve him faithfully. So has he been able to save you from the lions?"
—Daniel 6:20

Day 191

The king knew how strong Daniel's faith in God was. In the morning, he ran to see if his friend Daniel was safe. Daniel was alive! He wasn't even hurt. God had sent angels to hold the lions back. The king knew it was a miracle! The king praised the God of Daniel!

God's miracles are for everyone to see. They are God's way of showing his love and care.

I praise you, God, for caring about and loving all of us.

"My God sent his angel. And his angel shut the mouths of the lions. They haven't hurt me at all. That's because I haven't done anything wrong in God's sight. I've never done anything wrong to you either, Your Majesty."
—Daniel 6:22

Day 192

God sends his angels to watch over us!

When Daniel was thrown into the lions' den he was sure that everything was going to be fine. The king worried all night long. He hoped Daniel's God would protect his friend. In the morning, he checked on Daniel. God had sent an angel to close the lions' mouths. This angel was God's way of saying he believed in Daniel and loved him.

I know you will never fail me, O Lord.

"I order every part of my kingdom to respect and honor Daniel's God. He is the living God. He will live forever. His kingdom will not be destroyed. His rule will never end."
—Daniel 6:26

Day 193

King Darius saw how God had saved his friend Daniel. He wanted to know more about the God of Daniel. He wanted his people to worship God too. God's plan had worked! Now more people would come to know him. More people would see how much God loved and cared about them.

The king, who didn't even know God, ordered everyone in his kingdom to honor the God of Daniel! We should praise God for all of his works and words.

Your works and words are great, God!

*"Go to the great city of Nineveh. Preach against it.
The sins of its people have come to my attention."*
—Jonah 1:2

Day 194

God is sad when people do bad things. He loves all people and wants them to be sorry for their sins.

God really wanted Jonah to go to Nineveh. The people there were sinning a lot. Jonah was one of God's prophets. God wanted Jonah to teach the people about God's love and mercy. But Jonah did not want to go. He didn't like the people of Nineveh.

Help me go wherever you want me to go, God.

But Jonah ran away from the Lord. He headed for Tarshish. So he went down to the port of Joppa. There he found a ship that was going to Tarshish. He paid the fare and went on board. Then he sailed for Tarshish. He was running away from the LORD. —Jonah 1:3

Day 195

Sometimes we just do not want to listen to God. Sometimes it feels easier to walk away from God. Being good and doing the right thing all the time is not always easy or fun. That is how Jonah felt. He did not want to go to Nineveh so he ran away. But when God has a plan to us, we can't hide from him!

We can try to run away from God, but he always knows exactly where we are!

If I run away, help me find my way home, God.

But the Lord sent a strong wind over the Mediterranean Sea. A wild storm came up. It was so wild that the ship was in danger of breaking apart.
—Jonah 1:4

Day 196

Storms can be scary. There is rain and wind, loud thunder and lightning. When God sent a storm to the sea around Jonah's boat, the sailors were scared. God did not want to hurt them. He wanted Jonah to get his message loud and clear! God wanted Jonah to do his will.

God sometimes sends storms into our lives. He wants us to stop, think, and turn around!

If I am not listening, God, help me to hear. Help me be a better listener.

They found out he was running away from the L<small>ORD</small>. That's because he had told them. Then they became terrified. So they asked him, "How could you do a thing like that?"
—Jonah 1:10

Day 197

We need to keep our hearts open to God. Jonah knew that, but he forgot for a little while. When he saw the storm, he knew God was serious. Jonah knew God wanted him to do a job. He could not ignore God when so many people were in danger. Jonah knew what he had to do!

The sooner we realize what God is trying to tell us, the better!

God, open my heart and ears to your will.

Day 198

Jonah knew the storm was his fault. He told the men to toss him into the sea. God would protect the men.

Jonah knew he had to follow God's plan. He knew the storm was God's way of reminding him who was in charge! So Jonah told the sailors to toss him into the water. He promised the storm would stop. And it did stop! The sailors saw how powerful Jonah's God is!

Please help calm the storm around me, God.

Now the LORD sent a huge fish to swallow Jonah. And Jonah was in the belly of the fish for three days and three nights.
—Jonah 1:17

Day 199

God did not let Jonah drown in the sea! A huge fish came along and swallowed him. It was amazing. Jonah was inside the fish for three days and three nights. It must have been scary but Jonah knew that God was in charge. Jonah knew that God knew what he was doing!

God sent a big fish to rescue Jonah! God had a plan for Jonah. He has a plan for us too.

Thank you for the times you have rescued me, God.

The LORD gave the fish a command. And it spit Jonah up onto dry land.
—Jonah 2:10

Day 200

When Jonah was ready to obey God, God told the big fish to spit Jonah out.

Jonah spent his time inside the fish praying. He told God he was sorry. He promised to follow God's plan. God knew that Jonah was really sorry. He knew his prophet was ready to do God's work in Nineveh. Jonah was God's best man for the job. So God told the fish to spit Jonah out.

God, let me help spread your word!

A message from the LORD came to Jonah a second time.
—Jonah 3:1

Day 201

Jonah told God he was sorry. So God caused the big fish to spit Jonah out onto dry land. This time Jonah did what God wanted. He went to Nineveh. Jonah told the people of Nineveh about God and his love for them.

God gives us second chances!

Thanks for not giving up on us, God!

Jonah obeyed the LORD. He went to Nineveh. It was a very large city. In fact, it took about three days to go through it.
—Jonah 3:3

Day 202

Jonah was glad to be alive! He'd learned his lesson. He had a new attitude!

Jonah was thankful God had given him a chance to change his mind about going to Nineveh. He promised to share God's love. Jonah understood that God was serious about helping the people in Nineveh.

Can I help you like Jonah helped you, God?

God saw what they did. He saw that they stopped doing what was evil.
So he took pity on them. He didn't destroy them as he had said he would.
—Jonah 3:10

Day 203

Jonah told the people in Nineveh that God would destroy their city! They needed to start acting better. The people believed God's word and warning. They said they were sorry and would change their ways. The king heard God's word, and he changed too! God's plan was successful.

God forgave the people of Nineveh. He will forgive anyone who is really sorry! He forgives us.

Thank you, God, for your forgiveness and mercy!

The angel said to him, "I am Gabriel. I serve God.
I have been sent to speak to you and to tell you this good news."
—Luke 1:19

Day 204

Angels help
God's people. They
bring messages
from God.

Gabriel was a messenger for God. He spoke with Zechariah. Gabriel told Zechariah that Elizabeth, Mary's cousin, was going to have a baby! The baby was John the Baptist! It was great news for the world. It was happy news for Zechariah and Elizabeth.

I believe in angels, God.

... "The Lord has blessed you in a special way. He is with you."
—Luke 1:28

Day 205

Mary loved and trusted God. One day, an angel named Gabriel visited her. She was scared! But the angel told her not to be afraid. He said, "God has given you special favor. You will give birth to God's Son."

God sent his Son Jesus to earth to be with us and to save us from our sins.

Open my heart like Mary opened hers, God!

Mary said, "My soul gives glory to the Lord."
—Luke 1:46

Day 206

Remember that God can do anything!

Mary told the angel, "I'm not married yet. How can I have a baby?" Gabriel said, "With God, all things are possible." Mary believed it! She agreed to do what God was asking of her. She would become the mother of Jesus.

I am ready to do your will, God!

*"I serve the Lord," Mary answered. "May it happen to me
just as you said it would." Then the angel left her.*
—Luke 1:38

Day 207

Mary did not hesitate. She listened to the angel. Then she accepted what God said. She was willing to do the things God wanted! Mary's faith was amazing! How did she get so strong and brave? She knew God loved her and would take care of her, no matter what.

The best attitude is one that says "I will do anything you want me to, God."

Help me to be brave like Mary, God.

So Joseph went also. He went from the town of Nazareth in Galilee to Judea. That is where Bethlehem, the town of David, was. Joseph went there because he belonged to the family line of David. He went there with Mary to be listed. Mary was engaged to him. She was expecting a baby. —Luke 2:4–5

Day 208

Just because we love God doesn't mean we won't have hard times. God likes to challenge us.

Mary and Joseph knew that what they had to do would be hard. The angels that brought them messages did not say it would be easy. But they said it was God's will! Joseph and Mary had great faith. They relied on each other and on God's love and help.

I rely on you, God.

While Joseph and Mary were there, the time
came for the child to be born.
—Luke 2:6

Day 209

Mary and Joseph loved each other. In a dream, and angel told Joseph to make Mary his wife. So he did. They would follow God's plan together! But it wasn't easy. They couldn't even find a room in Bethlehem for Mary to have the baby.

Following God's plans is not always easy. But we must always try.

I will trust you all the time, God.

She gave birth to her first baby. It was a boy. She wrapped him in large strips of cloth. Then she placed him in a manger. That's because there was no guest room where they could stay.
—Luke 2:7

Day 210

The Savior of the world was born in the least expected place!

Jesus is the Son of God. He is God in human flesh! He is greater than the greatest king. Yet he was born in the lowest of places. Imagine a manger surrounded by hay and smelly animals. That's where Jesus was born. Jesus is a Savior for everyone!

God, happy birthday to your Son!

But the angel said to them, "Do not be afraid. I bring you good news. It will bring great joy for all the people."
—Luke 2:10

Day 211

Jesus was born as a little baby, just like you were. But his birth was the best news anyone could hear! Jesus would grow up and teach the whole world about God's love. Jesus came to save everyone from their sins.

> Jesus' birth was the most important news in the world.

Thank you for the best gift ever, God!

Suddenly a large group of angels from heaven also appeared. They were praising God.
—Luke 2:13

Day 212

Listen, God has a message for us too! Jesus was born for all of us!

On the night Jesus was born, some shepherds were out in the fields. Suddenly, they heard and saw angels! The angels told the shepherds about the birth of the Savior. Think about how happy they must have been!

Thank you for the good news of Jesus' birth, God!

An angel of the Lord appeared to them. And the glory of the Lord shone around them. They were terrified. But the angel said to them, "Do not be afraid. I bring you good news. It will bring great joy for all the people."
—Luke 2:9–10

Day 213

God's angels like to praise God! That is what God's angels did on the night Jesus was born ... they praised God and thanked him for loving the world so much! God had sent his Son to earth to teach about God's love. It was joyful news.

When Jesus was born, the angels in heaven were just as happy as the people on earth!

I will sing praises with the angels, God.

Day 214

God deserves
our very
best praise!

The angels said to the shepherds,
"Glory to God in the highest!"
They were giving great thanks
and praise to God for the good
news of Jesus' birth. God deserves
our very best praise. He deserves
our highest honor.

God, I give you great thanks and praise!

... Then the shepherds said to one another, "Let's go to Bethlehem. Let's see this thing that has happened, which the Lord has told us about."
—Luke 2:15

Day 215

The shepherds went to Bethlehem to see baby Jesus. They were so excited! Then they helped spread the news! They wanted everyone to know that Jesus was the Savior. The Savior had come to earth!

God wants us to be messengers for his good news.

I want to help spread your good news, God!

221

In Jerusalem there was a man named Simeon. He was a good and godly man. He was waiting for God's promise to Israel to come true.
—Luke 2:25

Day 216

Sometimes waiting can be hard. We can ask God for patience.

Simeon was a very old man. He loved God a lot. God told Simeon that he would not die before he had seen the Savior. One day, Simeon saw Mary and Joseph with baby Jesus. Simeon was filled with joy! He knew Jesus was the Savior.

Help me to be patient, God.

Anna came up to Jesus' family at that very moment. She gave thanks to God. And she spoke about the child to all who were looking forward to the time when Jerusalem would be set free.
—Luke 2:38

Day 217

Anna was 84 years old. She stayed at the temple all the time. She was praying and waiting for the Savior. She told many people he was coming. When Joseph and Mary brought baby Jesus to the temple, Anna knew he was God's Son!

God uses everyone to spread his good news.

God, Jesus truly is your Son!

Jesus was born in Bethlehem in Judea. This happened while Herod was king of Judea. After Jesus' birth, Wise Men from the east came to Jerusalem.
—Matthew 2:1

Day 218

The heavens showed off the good news of the birth of God's Son!

When Jesus was born, there was a special star in the sky. It was really bright. It let people near and faraway know that something special had happened. God wanted everyone to find out about the birth of his Son.

Thank you for the special star, God!

They asked, "Where is the child who has been born to be king of the Jews?
We saw his star when it rose. Now we have come to worship him."
—Matthew 2:2

Day 219

Three wise men lived in a faraway country. They saw the special star in the sky. They knew the star meant that a Savior was born. So they decided to follow the star. They traveled a long way. They wanted to find the Savior.

The Savior is for everyone, everywhere

Thank you for your guidance, God.

The Wise Men went to the house. They saw the child with his mother Mary. They bowed down and worshiped him. Then they opened their treasures. They gave him gold, frankincense and myrrh.
—Matthew 2:11

Day 220

The wise men brought expensive gifts to Jesus to honor him as King.

The star led the wise men to Jesus! They gave him gold, frankincense, and myrrh. These were very special gifts to give. The wise men knew how important Jesus was to the world. They knew Jesus was the King of Kings.

I give you my heart, God.

Day 221

The wise men visited Jesus and his parents. They showed Jesus their love and respect. But Jesus was in danger! So when it was time for the wise men to go back to their land, God sent a message through a dream. He told the wise men not to return to King Herod!

To protect his people, sometimes God speaks to people in dreams.

I love and respect you, Lord.

227

Day 222

Not everyone
wants to follow
King Jesus.
Open their
hearts, God!

Not everyone was happy about the birth of Jesus. King Herod was a mean man. When he heard that a new king was born, he was very mad! He wanted to be the only king. When the wise men did not return to him, he told his soldiers to find Jesus themselves.

Even when people do not love you,
I choose to love you, God!

When the Wise Men had left, Joseph had a dream. In the dream an angel of the Lord appeared to him. "Get up!" the angel said. "Take the child and his mother and escape to Egypt. Stay there until I tell you to come back. Herod is going to search for the child. He wants to kill him." —Matthew 2:13

Day 223

God knew Jesus might be in danger! So he warned Joseph and Mary. In a dream, an angel told Joseph to take Jesus to another country for a while. God would take care of their family. They listened to the angel.

If we listen, God will tell us exactly what to do. He knows what is best.

Take care of my family too, God!

Day 224

God never forgets. It might seem like a long time, but God always remembers.

Joseph and Mary and Jesus waited in Egypt a long time. But finally an angel told Joseph it was safe to leave. King Herod was dead. They could go to Israel again. Jesus would be safe back in his homeland!

Bless our home, God!

Every year Jesus' parents went to Jerusalem for the Passover Feast. When he was 12 years old, they went up to the Feast as usual.
—Luke 2:41–42

Day 225

Jesus was God, but he was a human being too. He grew up like us. He had a loving mother and father. They did family things together like play, work, travel, and pray. Jesus knows what children go through.

God's Son grew up just like all kids do! He was a lot like you and me.

God, help me be a good child like Jesus.

They thought he was somewhere in their group. So they traveled on for a day. Then they began to look for him among their relatives and friends.
—Luke 2:44

Day 226

Even as a young boy. Jesus wanted to be at the temple.

Jesus was God's Son. So Jesus went to the temple. It was his heavenly Father's house! But he forgot to tell Mary and Joseph. Mary and Joseph could not find Jesus. They were very worried about their boy.

Help me not to worry my parents, God!

They did not find him. So they went back to Jerusalem to look for him.
—Luke 2:45

Day 227

Jesus' parents had no idea where Jesus was. They needed to know he was safe. They looked everywhere. They refused to give up. Sometimes when we disobey God's rules, God wonders where we have gone. But God will not give up until we are home safe.

Parents won't give up looking when their child is lost. God feels that way about us!

I am safe with you, God.

*After three days they found him in the temple
courtyard. He was sitting with the teachers. He was
listening to them and asking them questions.*
—Luke 2:46

Day 228

You are never
too young to
talk about God!

When Jesus was a boy, he enjoyed
visiting the temple. He liked to talk
to teachers who knew a lot about
God. Jesus would listen and ask
questions. The teachers were amazed
that Jesus understood so much.

I want to know more about you, God!

"Why were you looking for me?" he asked.
"Didn't you know I had to be in my Father's house?"
—Luke 2:49

Day 229

A house of God is where we learn about and worship God. It is a very special place. Jesus liked being at the temple. He felt comfortable there. He loved to talk about and worship his Heavenly Father. He loved to talk about God's laws. He knew a lot about them.

We should love visiting God's house and learning all about God.

I want to learn everything I can about you, God!

He said, "Turn away from your sins!
The kingdom of heaven is near."
—Matthew 3:2

Day 230

God used helpers on earth to prepare the way for Jesus.

John the Baptist was Jesus' cousin. John loved God very much. He wanted to prepare the way for our Savior to come. So John told people that God was coming and they needed to prepare their hearts.

Am I ready for you, God?

When they confessed their sins, John baptized them in the Jordan.
—Matthew 3:6

Day 231

John taught people about God's love. He said they should turn away from their sins. If they did that, God would forgive them. Some people listened to John. They said they were sorry for their sins. They promised to love God. So John baptized them.

God wants people to get ready to follow Jesus.

I am sorry for my sins too, God.

When all the people were being baptized, Jesus was baptized too. And as he was praying, heaven was opened. The Holy Spirit came down on him in the form of a dove. A voice came from heaven. It said, "You are my Son, and I love you. I am very pleased with you." —Luke 3:21–22

Day 232

God the Father is please with his Son. He said so!

Jesus asked John to baptize him. John was very surprised! But John baptized Jesus anyway. God spoke from heaven and said that Jesus was his son and he was very pleased with Jesus. Then the Holy Spirit came down as a dove!

I want you to be pleased with me too, God.

From that time on Jesus began to preach. "Turn away from your sins!" he said. "The kingdom of heaven has come near."
—Matthew 4:17

Day 233

There is nobody else like Jesus. God sent him down from heaven. Jesus had a big job to do. He had to tell people all about God and how much God loved them. It is amazing that God would want us to know him!

Jesus came to tell us about God, his heavenly Father.

I am sorry for my sins too, God.

"Come and follow me," Jesus said.
"I will send you out to fish for people."
—Matthew 4:19

Day 234

Jesus needed helpers to spread his Father's message of love. Jesus lets us help him too!

Jesus knew teaching about God was a big job. There were so many people to tell! Jesus wanted helpers. He looked for helpers who were happy to do hard work. He found some fishermen and said, "Follow me."

I am not afraid to work hard for you, God!

As Jesus went on from there, he saw a man named Matthew.
He was sitting at the tax collector's booth. "Follow me,"
Jesus told him. Matthew got up and followed him.
—Matthew 9:9

Day 235

Some people did not like the tax man named Matthew. But Jesus knew Matthew would be a good helper. So Jesus asked him to help teach about God. Matthew quit his tax job so he could help Jesus!

Sometimes God surprises us with whom he asks to come and help.

Help me to see good in everyone, God.

Jesus went up on a mountainside. He called for certain people to come to him, and they came.
—Mark 3:13

Day 236

Jesus knew he needed strong and faithful helpers. Jesus wants us to be good followers too.

Jesus picked twelve men to be his special helpers. They were ordinary men. They were not famous men. Jesus didn't pick them because of how they looked or how smart or rich they were. Jesus just knew they would be good followers.

Keep me strong and faithful, God.

Day 237

Jesus, his mother Mary, and his friends were at a wedding. When the wine ran out, his mother heard about it. She told the servants, "Do what Jesus tells you to do." She wanted Jesus to do a miracle!

God knew Jesus was ready to show God's love with a miracle. There are miracles all around us!

God, I believe you do miracles every day!

What Jesus did here in Cana in Galilee was the first of his signs. Jesus showed his glory by doing this sign. And his disciples believed in him.
—John 2:11

Day 238

Jesus does miracles to teach people about God's love.

Jesus told the servants to fill up some jugs with water. Then he told them to dip some out into a cup and take it to their master. They did what he said. When the master took a sip, it wasn't water. It was wine. It was a miracle!

Thank you for miracles, God!

Jesus saw the crowds. So he went up on a mountainside and sat down. His disciples came to him.
—Matthew 5:1

Day 239

Jesus was a great teacher. He taught men and women, boys and girls. People of all ages came to hear him. He used stories and ideas that people understood. Jesus loved his heavenly Father and knew exactly what to say.

God wants everyone to hear and understand his message.

I will listen to Jesus' teaching, God.

"If that is how God dresses the wild grass, how much better will he dress you! After all, the grass is here only today. Tomorrow it is thrown into the fire. Your faith is so small!"
—Luke 12:28

Day 240

God makes the flowers of the field beautiful and bloom. So we don't have to worry. He will take care of our needs too!

God never ignores us and what we need. We were created in his image, so we are very special to him. God does not want us to worry about things like food and clothes. God knows just what we need. He gives that to us, and more!

Thank you for taking such good care of me.

"Aren't five sparrows sold for two pennies? But God does not forget even one of them. In fact, he even counts every hair on your head! So don't be afraid. You are worth more than many sparrows."
—Luke 12:6–7

Day 241

Jesus taught the people about God's love. He said God would love them forever. God cares so much about us! He even knows how many hairs are on our heads. He loves us that much! We should not have any worries.

God cares for us more than we can imagine!

Thank you for loving me so much, God!

x

247

"This is how you should pray.
"'Our Father in heaven, may your name be honored.'"
—Matthew 6:9

Day 242

There are many ways that we can tell God we love him. One way is to pray.

Jesus taught the people many things. He taught them about prayer. Jesus prayed, and he wanted the people to pray too. One day, he taught them a prayer. We call it "The Lord's Prayer." People can pray this prayer every day.

Talking with you helps me, God.

Day 243

Everyone wanted to see Jesus. Big crowds came to him. Jesus helped many, many people. But he did not help everyone. He prayed and asked his Heavenly Father which needs he should meet. He knew his disciples would help more people in the future.

Jesus healed lots of people, but he didn't have time to meet every single need. He wants helpers!

If I can help you, please use me.

249

The commander replied, "Lord, I am not good enough to have you come into my house. But just say the word, and my servant will be healed."
—Matthew 8:8

Day 244

Some people are filled with faith in God. God wants us to be filled with faith too.

An army captain asked Jesus to help his sick servant. Jesus wanted to go to the captain's house to heal the man. But the captain said, "Just say the word and he will be fine." Jesus was amazed that the captain had such great faith in him.

Fill me with faith, God.

Then Jesus said to the Roman commander, "Go! It will be done just as you believed it would." And his servant was healed at that moment.
—Matthew 8:13

Day 245

The captain believed Jesus could heal his servant without being there. Jesus said, "Go! It will be done as you believed it would." The captain was right! The servant was healed just because Jesus said the word.

God rewards our faith.

Please make my faith strong like the captain's, God.

Day 246

People came to Jesus ready to listen to what he had to say!

People followed Jesus everywhere. They were so excited to see him. People loved listening to him talk! He told them all about God's love. They wanted to hear everything Jesus had to say. The people came to him with open hearts and open ears.

Help me to hear!

So some men came carrying a man who could not walk.
He was lying on a mat. They tried to take him into the
house to place him in front of Jesus.
—Luke 5:18

Day 247

Jesus was teaching inside a house. It was too crowded to fit anyone else. A man who lived nearby could not walk. His friends believed Jesus could heal him. They made a hole in the roof. They wanted to get their friend to Jesus!

It is good to have faith-filled friends who help us.

I am thankful for my good friends, God!

When Jesus saw that they had faith he spoke to the man.
He said, "Friend, your sins are forgiven."
—Luke 5:20

Day 248

Jesus will hear and answer the prayers of our friends too.

Jesus saw how much the four men loved their friend. They believed God could heal their friend. Jesus liked their faith. He wanted to help the man walk. Jesus forgave his sins. The man stood up all by himself! It was a miracle!

I feel free when I know my sin is forgiven by you, God.

It was very early in the morning and still dark. Jesus got up and left the house. He went to a place where he could be alone. There he prayed.
—Mark 1:35

Day 249

Prayer was important to Jesus. He loved talking with his heavenly Father. No matter how tired or busy he was, Jesus always spent time praying. Jesus wants us to pray too. He teaches us how to pray. And we have many great reasons to pray.

> Jesus took special time out to pray. We should do that too.

Thanks for being someone I can always talk to.

One day Jesus said to his disciples, "Let's go over to the other side of the lake." So they got into a boat and left. As they sailed, Jesus fell asleep ...
—Luke 8:22–23

Day 250

Even though he was God, Jesus took time out to rest from his work. We should too.

Sometimes we forget that even though Jesus is God's Son, here on earth he was also human! He needed to rest and relax just like we do. Jesus worked very hard teaching people and his disciples. Jesus deserved to rest. He knew rest was good for him.

Help me rest secure, knowing you are here.

Jesus got into a boat. His disciples followed him.
Suddenly a terrible storm came up on the lake. The
waves crashed over the boat. But Jesus was sleeping.
—Matthew 8:23–24

Day 251

It was time for Jesus and his helpers to go across the sea. They got into a boat. Jesus took a nap. Suddenly, there was a really big storm! Jesus' helpers were scared. They thought the boat was going to sink.

We have to trust in the Lord even when times get rough.

I should not fear the storm with you nearby, God!

He replied, "Your faith is so small! Why are you so afraid?"
—Matthew 8:26a

Day 252

Even the most faithful forget sometimes.

Jesus' helpers were upset. The storm was scary. They woke up Jesus and shouted, "The boat is sinking! Don't you care?" Jesus said, "Why are you so afraid? Don't you have any faith?" Then Jesus told the storm to stop.

I know you understand my fears, God.

Then Jesus got up and ordered the winds and the waves to stop. It became completely calm.
—Matthew 8:26b

Day 253

When Jesus told the storm to stop, the water became calm. The storm was gone! The disciples couldn't believe it. It was a miracle! Everyone was safe. Jesus was right. With him in the boat, they had nothing to fear.

Relax and know that we are safe with Jesus.

You truly are the Savior, Jesus!

While Jesus was saying this, a synagogue leader came. He got down on his knees in front of Jesus. He said, "My daughter has just died. But come and place your hand on her. Then she will live again."
—Matthew 9:18

Day 254

Jesus teaches us to be faithful. He wants us to trust him completely.

A leader named Jairus needed Jesus' help. His little girl was sick. Jairus knew that all Jesus had to do was touch her. Then his daughter would be fine. Jesus knew that Jairus was filled with faith. He went with Jairus.

Jesus, I believe you can help with anything.

He said, "Go away. The girl is not dead.
She is sleeping." But they laughed at him.
—Matthew 9:24

Day 255

Jesus walked home with Jairus. But when they got there, it was bad news. The people told Jairus that his little girl had died. Jairus' strong faith was not so strong anymore. But Jesus was there for Jairus. "Trust me," Jesus said.

Sometimes bad things happen. Then it is hard to keep believing.

Sometimes I have trouble with my faith, God.

While Jesus was still speaking, some people came from the house of Jairus. He was the synagogue leader. "Your daughter is dead," they said. "Why bother the teacher anymore?" Jesus heard what they were saying. He told the synagogue ruler, "Don't be afraid. Just believe." —Mark 5:35–36

Day 256

It is never too late for God! Nothing is impossible for God to make happen.

Jesus told Jairus to trust him. Jairus wanted to trust Jesus. He knew that if anyone could help his daughter, Jesus was the one! But it was hard to trust because Jairus had heard that his daughter was dead. But with God's love it is never too late if we believe!

I see miracles all around. Thank you!

After the crowd had been sent outside, Jesus went in.
He took the girl by the hand, and she got up.
—Matthew 9:25

Day 257

Jesus went to see the little girl. He held her hand. Even though she was dead, Jesus told her to get up. She did! Jairus and his wife were so happy. Even when their faith was not strong, God understood. And he helped their daughter.

Jesus will never let us down. His faith hold ours up.

Help my faith wake up like Jairus' little girl, God.

Just then a woman came up behind Jesus. She had a sickness that made her bleed. It had lasted for 12 years. She touched the edge of his clothes.
—Matthew 9:20

Day 258

Jesus wants us to be closer to him.

There was a huge crowd around Jesus. In the crowd was a really sick lady. She had been sick for twelve years. The doctors couldn't heal her. She didn't give up. She had to get to Jesus! She knew if she could just touch his clothes, she would be healed.

Help me get closer to you, Lord.

Jesus turned and saw her. "Dear woman, don't give up hope," he said. "Your faith has healed you." The woman was healed at that moment.
—Matthew 9:22

Day 259

The sick lady pushed through the crowd. Finally, she was close enough! She reached out and touched Jesus' clothes. In that second, she was healed! Jesus turned to the lady. He was so proud of her strong faith. He said, "Go in peace!"

Don't let anything stop you from reaching out to Jesus.

Help me reach out to you, God.

"This is how it will be on judgment day. The angels will come. They will separate the people who did what is wrong from those who did what is right."
—Matthew 13:49

Day 260

God knows the difference between good people and evil people.

Jesus told a story about some fishermen who caught a lot of fish. The fishermen looked at each one. They kept the good ones. They tossed out the bad ones. That's what God will do. He will pick out the good people to live with him in heaven forever and not include the bad ones.

I want to live with you forever, God.

But many people were coming and going. So they did not even have a chance to eat. Then Jesus said to his apostles, "Come with me by yourselves to a quiet place. You need to get some rest."
—Mark 6:31

Day 261

Jesus and his disciples were worn out. People had followed them and listened to Jesus all day long. He had preached. He had healed people. He had listened to people. Jesus needed a break. So Jesus and his friends got into a boat and pushed off into the water.

Even Jesus and his disciples got tired. We all need to rest sometimes.

Jesus, help me rest when I need to.

By that time it was late in the day. His disciples came to him. "There is nothing here," they said. "It's already very late. Send the people away. They can go to the nearby countryside and villages to buy something to eat." —Mark 6:35–36

Day 262

People are hungry for food. But people are hungrier to hear about God's love.

Over 5,000 people had come to see Jesus. He helped and healed many of them. The people were hungry and tired. But the people did not want to go home. Jesus' helpers were worried. They said, "It's time for dinner. The people should go home and eat."

Jesus, I am hungry to hear about God's love.

"Here is a boy with five small loaves of barley bread. He also has two small fish. But how far will that go in such a large crowd?"
—John 6:9

Day 263

Jesus said, "See if anyone has food to share." The disciples found a boy with two fish and five loaves of bread to share. They took the boy to Jesus. Jesus blessed the fish and bread. The disciples started to pass the food out to the people.

God wants us to be willing to share.

Help me share with others, God.

So they gathered what was left over from the five barley loaves. They filled 12 baskets with the pieces left by those who had eaten. The people saw the sign that Jesus did. Then they began to say, "This must be the Prophet who is supposed to come into the world." —John 6:13–14

Day 264

There is always enough with Jesus. He makes sure that each of us has what we need and more.

The disciples gave bread and fish to the people. It was incredible! There was more than enough for everyone. All the people were full, and there were twelve baskets of food left over. It was a miracle!

Jesus, you give us everything we need.

After he had sent them away, he went up on a mountainside
by himself to pray. Later that night, he was there alone.
—Matthew 14:23

Day 265

No matter how busy he was, Jesus loved talking to his heavenly Father. One day, Jesus told his friends to go away for a while. He wanted to pray alone. He would follow them later. The friends went to their boat. Jesus went to a quiet place to pray.

Jesus needed to talk to God, just like we do.

I love talking to you, God!

Shortly before dawn, Jesus went out to the disciples. He walked on the lake.
—Matthew 14:25

Day 266

Jesus did amazing miracles. Amazing miracles happen today too!

While Jesus was praying, his helpers were in their boat. A big storm came. It was raining hard. It was so windy! The disciples were very scared. Then they saw something amazing. Jesus was walking to them. He was walking on the water!

Thank you, God, for signs that show us you are with us.

Day 267

The disciples thought Jesus was a ghost! Jesus' friend Peter needed proof. He said, "If you are Jesus, I want to walk on water too." Jesus said, "Come." So Peter got out of the boat. He walked on the water to Jesus.

We can believe amazing things if we have faith and open our hearts.

Help me to believe in you, God.

But when Peter saw the wind, he was afraid. He began to sink.
He cried out, "Lord! Save me!" Right away Jesus reached out his hand
and caught him. "Your faith is so small!" he said. "Why did you doubt me?"
—Matthew 14:30–31

Day 268

Jesus' helping hand is always there to pull us up.

Even when Peter doubted him, Jesus still came to his rescue! Jesus was like that. He loved no matter what. He cared no matter what. Jesus showed how perfect God's love is for us. Jesus supports us through good and bad. He will always reach out to us if we ask.

Thank you for supporting me.

When they climbed into the boat, the wind died down. Then those in the boat worshiped Jesus. They said, "You really are the Son of God!"
—Matthew 14:32–33

Day 269

When Peter looked at the wind and the waves, he started to sink. "Why didn't you trust me?" Jesus asked Peter. Jesus helped Peter get back in the boat. Then the storm stopped. Jesus' disciples said, "Truly you are the Son of God!"

Jesus wants us to trust him. Sometimes it might be hard. But he still wants us to try!

Jesus, you are the Son of God!

*As Jesus went along, he saw a man who was blind. He had been blind since he was born. Jesus'
disciples asked him, "Rabbi, who sinned? Was this man born blind because he sinned? Or did
his parents sin?" "It isn't because this man sinned," said Jesus. "It isn't because his parent
sinned. He was born blind so that God's power could be shown by what's going to happen."
—John 9:1–3*

Day 270

Jesus is very
compassionate.
That means he
cares a lot
about people!

Again and again, Jesus showed
how much he loved people. He
wanted to teach people about his
father's love. Every chance he had,
Jesus helped, taught, supported, and
blessed people in the name of his
heavenly Father. He cared about
people's pain.

Bless me, Father!

276

As Jesus went along, he saw a man who was blind.
He had been blind since he was born.
—John 9:1

Day 271

Jesus and his helpers saw a blind man. The man was asking people for food or money. Jesus went to the blind man. He made some mud and put it on the man's eyes. "Go to the pool. Wash the mud off," Jesus told the man.

> Jesus cares about poor people. He wants us to care about them too.

Jesus, I want to be caring just like you.

277

Jesus said, "You have now seen him. In fact, he is the one speaking with you." Then the man said, "Lord, I believe." And he worshiped him.
—John 9:37–38

Day 272

When Jesus did miracles, people wanted to know more about him.

The blind man felt silly with mud on his eyes. But he did what Jesus said. He went to the pool and washed his face. As soon as the mud was gone, he could see! Everyone was amazed. They all wanted to find out more about Jesus.

Jesus, help me see you clearly like the blind man did!

Jesus and his disciples arrived in Capernaum. There the people who collect the temple tax came to Peter. They asked him, "Doesn't your teacher pay the temple tax?"
—Matthew 17:24

Day 273

Taxes were important. They helped pay for fixing up the temple. One day, some tax collectors asked Peter if Jesus paid his taxes. Jesus was the Son of God, so he didn't have to pay. But he did it anyway!

Even though he is the Son of God, Jesus still obeyed men's laws.

Help me accept my responsibilities, Lord.

" ... So go to the lake and throw out your fishing line. Take the first fish you catch. Open its mouth. There you will find the exact coin you need. Take it and give it to them for my tax and yours."
—Matthew 17:27

Day 274

Jesus helps us with the little things. He helps us with the big things too.

Jesus told Peter to go catch a fish. He said there would be money in the mouth of the fish. Sure enough, there was! It was just the right amount to pay the taxes for Jesus and Peter. It was a miracle!

Thank you, Jesus, for helping with our needs.

*He answered, "Love the Lord your God with all your heart and
with all your soul. Love him with all your strength and with
all your mind.' And, 'Love your neighbor as you love yourself.'"*
—Luke 10:27

Day 275

One day, a man said to Jesus, "I know I have to love God. I have to love my neighbor too. But who is my neighbor?" Jesus told a story about a man who was beaten up by robbers and left by the side of the road.

> **Jesus helps me to understand who I should take care of. Everyone is my neighbor!**

I will love my neighbor the best I can.

Day 276

Jesus says to love your neighbor as you love yourself. Sometimes that is hard to do!

A man was robbed and hurt. He needed help. Two men passed right by him. They did not stop to see if they could help. Then another man came by. He was a Samaritan. He felt sorry for the hurt man and helped him. He was the man's true neighbor.

Help me know what to do in hard situations, God.

Day 277

The Samaritan was a caring person. He did not just leave the hurt man to get better. He took him to an inn. He paid the innkeeper to look after the man. He even went back to check on him. The Samaritan man shows us how to love our neighbors.

Being a good neighbor is an important job! God blesses good neighbors.

Thank you for good people who help us, God.

... Mary sat at the Lord's feet listening to what he said.
—Luke 10:39

Day 278

Jesus likes it when we sit and listen to him.

Jesus had some good friends named Mary and Martha. They were sisters. Jesus visited Mary and Martha when he could. On one visit, Mary sat with Jesus. He told her about God's love. She was happy sitting with him, listening to his message.

Jesus, I want to be a good friend to you like Mary was.

But Martha was busy with all the things that had to be done.
—Luke 10:40

Day 279

While Mary was sitting and listening to Jesus, Martha was racing around the house. She was cooking and cleaning. She was busy getting everything ready for Jesus! Martha was so busy that she didn't spend time with Jesus.

Sometimes it is hard to relax and enjoy Jesus. But we need to!

Help me take the time to relax and enjoy you, Lord.

"But few things are needed. Really, only one thing is needed. Mary has chosen what is better. And it will not be taken away from her."
—Luke 10:42

Day 280

> Jesus wants us to listen to his words. He wants us to be still and learn about his Father's love.

Martha was angry. She was upset that Mary wasn't helping her. Jesus said, "Martha, you should not be upset. Mary has chosen what is better." Mary chose to listen to Jesus over working hard.

I choose you, Jesus.

Day 281

People came to hear Jesus. They wanted to know who was most important to God. Jesus told the people a story. It was about a shepherd. Shepherds get food and water for their sheep. They keep the sheep safe. They love each one of their sheep.

> **Jesus used special stories called parables to help people understand God's love.**

God, thank you for taking care of us like a shepherd.

*He said, "Suppose one of you has 100 sheep and loses
one of them. Won't he leave the 99 in the open country?
Won't he go and look for the one lost sheep until he finds it?"*
—Luke 15:4

Day 282

Everyone on earth
is equal in God's
eyes. He loves
us all the same.

God loves everyone. He loves short
and tall and rich and poor and young
and old people. He loves people from
every nation. He wants us all to love
him too. Once you are part of God's
family, he does not let you get lost!

Thank you, God, for letting me be part of your family!

"When he finds it, he will joyfully put it on his shoulders ..."
—Luke 15:5

Day 283

A shepherd doesn't want even one sheep to be lost and alone. He want them all safe and sound. He wants them with his flock. He will leave his flock to find a missing sheep and bring it back home. He cares about each sheep that much!

When we sin and lose our way, God will do all he can to get us back.

Thank you for finding me, God.

Jesus continued, "There was a man who had two sons. The younger son spoke to his father. He said, 'Father, give me my share of the family property.' So the father divided his property between his two sons."
—Luke 15:11–12

Day 284

God lets us make our own choices. Some choices are good and some choices are not.

Jesus told the people a story. It was about a man and his two sons. They lived on a farm. The younger son did not like to work. He asked for some money. When he got the money, he packed up his suitcase. He chose to go away from his family.

Guide the choices I make every day. God.

"Not long after that, the younger son packed up all he had. Then he left for a country far away."
—Luke 15:13

Day 285

The son packed up his things. He wanted to leave home. He did not really think about what could happen. He just wanted to have fun. He thought he knew everything. But he didn't. We need God, the Bible, our parents, and God's friends to help us make good decisions.

Sometimes we can be making a big mistake and not even know it.

Help me understand that I do not know best all the time, God.

"He spent everything he had. Then the whole country ran low on food. So the son didn't have what he needed."
—Luke 15:14

Day 286

Even when we make a mistake, God loves us. He wants us to realize we were wrong.

The son did not make good choices. He did not pay attention to his money. He did not think about what his father might say to do. He did not think about what the Bible said he should do. He wanted to make his own decisions. So his problem grew bigger than it should have.

Help me accept responsibility for what I do, God.

"The son wanted to fill his stomach with the food the pigs were eating. But no one gave him anything."
—Luke 15:16

Day 287

The son knew he had to do something. He could not live without help. He needed money and food. He was not sure how to fix his problem. Then he realized he had to do the very thing he did not want to do. He had to get a job! He was sad. He missed his father's love.

> **Making bad choices will lead us into tough situations.**

Help me to never forget your love, Father.

"Then he began to think clearly again. He said, 'How many of my father's hired workers have more than enough food! But here I am dying from hunger!'"
—Luke 15:17

Day 288

It is a good idea to stop and think. Pray and ask God for help. He always knows what is best.

The son had made a bad choice to leave home. Now he was in trouble. He needed to think about what was best. When we do not think about our choices there can be problems! So the son sat down. He thought about what he should do next.

Thank you for your wisdom, God.

"The son said to him, 'Father, I have sinned against heaven and against you. I am no longer fit to be called your son.'"
—Luke 15:21

Day 289

The son had a plan. He would go home. He would apologize to his father. He would ask for a job. This would be very hard! He had to admit that he had made a bad choice. But the son knew going back was the right choice this time. He did not want to hurt his father or God anymore.

It might not be easy to do the right thing, but it is still the right thing to do!

When I make a mistake, please accept my apology. God. 295

"'This son of mine was dead. And now he is alive again. He was lost. And now he is found.' So they began to celebrate."
—Luke 15:24

Day 290

God welcomes us back when we are sorry.

The son went home. His father saw him coming! He was so happy. The son was sorry and his father forgave him! Then the father threw a big party for his son. God is like that too. He is so happy when we say we are sorry for our sins. He welcomes us back every time.

Thank you for loving me no matter what, God.

"'But we had to celebrate and be glad. This brother of yours was dead. And now he is alive again. He was lost. And now he is found.'"
—Luke 15:32

Day 291

When the son got home, his father was so happy! He forgave his son for his bad choices. The father had been hoping and waiting for his son to come home. He loved his son so much. So the father thew a big party for his son. The son was so happy to be back at home.

> There's no place like home! We should be grateful for our families.

Help me to remember how much my parents love me, God.

And they called out in a loud voice,
"Jesus! Master! Have pity on us!"
—Luke 17:13

Day 292

We all need
help sometimes.
We can always
go to Jesus.

Many people asked Jesus for help. One day, ten men went to Jesus. They had heard Jesus helped sick people. They had a skin disease called leprosy. It made sores all over their bodies. The men asked Jesus to make the sores go away.

When I need you, I know I can go to you, God.

Jesus saw them and said, "Go. Show yourselves to the priests."
While they were on the way, they were healed.
—Luke 17:14

Day 293

Jesus cared about the ten men. He knew they needed his help. Jesus healed them! The ten men took their bandages off. The sores were gone! It was a miracle. The men were amazed. They were so happy.

Jesus can heal us!

I know that God makes anything possible.

When one of them saw that he was healed, he came back.
He praised God in a loud voice.
—Luke 17:15

Day 294

Be like Jesus.
Share God's
goodness with
others.

All the men felt great! Jesus told them to go show the priests. Nine men rushed away. They were so excited. The men wanted to see their families and friends. They wanted to go back home.

God, true joy comes from knowing you and your love.

Jesus asked, "Weren't all ten healed? Where are the other nine?"
—Luke 17:17

Day 295

Nine men went running off. But one man turned back to Jesus. The man felt great. He was filled with joy. Before he ran off, he had to do one thing. "Thank you so much!" he told Jesus. Jesus wondered why only one man came to thank him.

Saying thank you is very important. We should not forget to thank God!

Do not let me forget to thank you, God.

People were bringing little children to Jesus. They wanted him to place his hands on them to bless them.
—Mark 10:13

Day 296

Jesus loves everyone. He loves old people and young people.

Jesus loved being with people. He was a good friend. He was a good teacher. Children everywhere could tell. Jesus never ignored them. He loved them. Jesus treated them like they were important too.

God, I know Jesus loves everyone!

When Jesus saw this, he was angry. He said to his disciples,
"Let the little children come to me. Don't keep them away."
—Mark 10:14

Day 297

Jesus was very busy. So his helpers told some children not to bother Jesus. The helpers thought they knew best. The children were sad. They turned away to go home. But Jesus called the children back. He wanted them to be with him.

Jesus is never too tired or too busy for us.

Thank you, Jesus, that you are never too tired for me.

"What I'm about to tell you is true. Anyone who will not receive God's kingdom like a little child will never enter it."
—Luke 10:15

Day 298

Jesus wants adults to have faith like little children!

Jesus loves all people. But he especially loves children. He likes their faith in him. He told his disciples to let the children come to him. Then he said something surprising. He said that adults should become like little children.

Thank you for loving all your children, God!

Zacchaeus wanted to see who Jesus was. But he was a short man. He could not see Jesus because of the crowd.
—Luke 19:3

Day 299

Jesus worked hard. He walked many miles. He taught lots of people about God. There were crowds of people around Jesus all the time. One man named Zacchaeus wanted to see and hear Jesus. But he was too short. So he climbed a tree!

Don't let anything stop you from hearing Jesus' words!

Help me do whatever I can to hear you, Lord.

Jesus reached the spot where Zacchaeus was. He looked up and said, "Zacchaeus, come down at once. I must stay at your house today."
—Luke 19:5

Day 300

Jesus accepts all people. He accepted Zacchaeus. He accepts you too.

Jesus saw Zacchaeus. There he was, up a tree! Jesus wanted to meet Zacchaeus. Jesus wanted to talk with him. The other people were surprised. They didn't like Zacchaeus. He collected tax money for the king. But Jesus still wanted to go to Zacchaeus' house.

Thank you, Jesus, for loving me!

So Zacchaeus came down at once and welcomed him gladly.
All the people saw this. They began to whisper among themselves.
They said, "Jesus has gone to be the guest of a sinner."
—Luke 19:6–7

Day 301

The crowds were not happy. Why was Jesus talking to Zacchaeus? He was not a good man. Jesus was going to visit Zacchaeus' house. Zacchaeus came down from the tree. He was so happy. Jesus cared about him too!

Jesus did not care about what was popular. He cares about people, no matter what.

Thanks for caring, Jesus.

Jesus said to Zaccheus, "Today salvation has come to your house."
—Luke 19:9

Day 302

When we are
sorry for our sins.
Jesus is happy.
I am sorry, Lord.

Zacchaeus was so happy. Jesus wanted to come to his house! Zacchaeus told Jesus he was sorry for his sins. He told Jesus he would do better. He would give money to the poor. He would even give back money he stole!

I want to make you happy. Jesus.

So the sisters sent a message to Jesus. "Lord,"
they told him, "the one you love is sick."
—John 11:3

Day 303

Jesus was teaching. He was
telling many people about God.
Then he got a letter. It was from
his friends Martha and Mary. Martha
and Mary needed Jesus. Their
brother, Jesus' friend Lazarus, was
very sick. They wanted Jesus to
come see Lazarus.

**Jesus is never
too busy for
his friends.**

When I do not feel well, I need your comfort, God.

"Lord," Martha said to Jesus, "I wish you had been here!
Then my brother would not have died."
—John 11:21

Day 304

Jesus is compassionate. He has loving feelings for us.

Jesus finished teaching. Then he went to see his friends. It was a long walk, but Jesus knew his friends needed him. When Jesus got there, Martha ran out to meet him. She had bad news. She was crying. Lazarus was dead. Jesus was so sad. He cried.

Help me to comfort friends that need me.

Jesus said to her, "I am the resurrection and the life.
Anyone who believes in me will live, even if they die."
—John 11:25

Day 305

Jesus was sad. But he knew what to do. He started to pray to his heavenly Father. Jesus asked God for help. He wanted Lazarus to live. He wanted Martha and Mary to feel better. So Jesus asked God to show his great love to the people.

When things seem very hard, we should turn to God for help.

When something seems too sad, help me turn to you and your love, God.

Then Jesus said, "Didn't I tell you that if you believe,
you would see God's glory?"
—John 11:40

Day 306

Sometimes people need help to believe in God's love. Miracles help people see God's love.

Jesus prayed to God for help. Then he called, "Lazarus! Come out!" Suddenly, Lazarus came out of the tomb! He was alive. It was a miracle! Many people saw him. They were amazed. Jesus had raised Lazarus from the dead! The people praised God.

I praise you, God. You are amazing.

A dinner was given at Bethany to honor Jesus.
Martha served the food ...
—John 12:2

Day 307

Jesus went to see his friends Martha, Mary, and Lazarus. Jesus knew he was always welcome in their home. They loved Jesus, and he loved them. Jesus was happy. It felt good for him to know that he was welcome to visit and stay.

Always be welcoming to God. He wants our love.

You are always welcome in my heart, God.

Then Mary took about a pint of pure nard. It was an expensive perfume. She poured it on Jesus' feet and wiped them with her hair. The house was filled with the sweet smell of the perfume.
—John 12:3

Day 308

No gift is too expensive to give to Jesus.

While Jesus was vising, Mary did something special. She wanted to show Jesus just how special he was. Mary took some expensive perfume. She poured it on Jesus' feet. She dried Jesus' feet with her hair!

How can I show you my love, God?

"Why wasn't this perfume sold? Why wasn't the money given to poor people? It was worth a year's pay."
—John 12:5

Day 309

One of Jesus' helpers saw Mary pour perfume on Jesus' feet. The helper was upset! He wanted to know why she had wasted so much money. It could have gone to the poor. But Jesus told him why. He said Mary did the right thing. She was giving Jesus honor.

I want to show others how much I love God. Help me teach others about you.

Help me give you honor every chance I get, Lord.

"If anyone says anything to you, say that the Lord needs them. The owner will send them right away."
—Matthew 21:3

Day 310

Because Jesus is God, he knows about things before they happen.

It was a special time of year called Passover. Jesus and his helpers were on their way to Jerusalem. Jesus told two of his helpers to go ahead. He wanted a donkey. He told the helpers exactly where they would find one.

Help me remember you always know what is going to happen, God.

"Say to the city of Zion, 'See, your king comes to you. He is gentle and riding on a donkey. He is riding on a donkey's colt.'"
—Matthew 21:5

Day 311

Usually kings rode donkeys. Jesus rode a donkey into Jerusalem. The people welcomed Jesus like a king! They waved and smiled. Jesus waved and smiled back. He blessed the people as he passed.

Jesus deserves to be treated like a king.

You are the one true King!

A very large crowd spread their coats on the road. Others cut branches from the trees and spread them on the road.
—Matthew 21:8

Day 312

From the time of his birth, Jesus was the one true King of Glory.

Jesus rode into the city. The people cheered. They cried out in praise to God. They shouted, "Hosanna!" Palm branches were waved in the air. People put branches and cloaks on the ground in front of Jesus and the donkey.

Jesus, you are the King of Glory!

The crowds answered, "This is Jesus. He is the
prophet from Nazareth in Galilee."
—Matthew 21:11

Day 313

Jesus was in the city of Jerusalem. Some leaders in Jerusalem were not happy. They did not like Jesus. They did not believe he was the King. They saw how the people loved Jesus. The leaders were jealous. They wanted to stop Jesus.

Some people do not like the idea of Jesus being the one true king.

Jesus, I know that you are the King!

Jesus sat down across from the place where people put their temple offerings. He watched the crowd putting their money into the offering boxes. Many rich people threw large amounts into them.
—Matthew 12:41

Day 314

Jesus sees what is inside our hearts.

Jesus and his helpers went to the temple. Jesus watched people putting money in a box. Some were rich. Some were poor. Rich people gave lots of money. But they were not really making a sacrifice. They still had lots more money.

Help me understand what it means to sacrifice, God.

Jesus asked his disciples to come to him. He said, "What I'm about to tell you is true. That poor widow has put more into the offering box than all the others. They all gave a lot because they're rich. But she gave even though she is poor. She put in everything she had. She gave all she had to live on." —Mark 12:43–44

Day 315

Jesus told his helpers to watch a poor widow. She had two small coins. She put them in the box for the temple. It was all the money she had! Jesus said she put in more than all the other people did. She gave everything she had. It was a true sacrifice.

Jesus knows when we sacrifice a lot. He knows what is in our hearts.

Help me to be more like the poor widow, God.

... Jesus loved his disciples who were in the world.
So he now loved them to the very end.
—John 13:1

Day 316

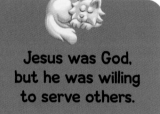

Jesus was God,
but he was willing
to serve others.

It was time for a special celebration called Passover. Jesus and his disciples would share a meal. Jesus knew he had to leave soon. So before they ate, Jesus did something special for his friends. He got towels and water. He wanted to wash his friends' feet!

God, help me to be a good friend like Jesus.

"I, your Lord and Teacher, have washed your feet. So you also should wash one another's feet. I have given you an example. You should do as I have done for you."
—John 13:14–15

Day 317

Even though he was God, Jesus washed each of the disciples' feet. His friend Peter wanted Jesus to stop. But Jesus said he had to do it. Jesus wanted them to understand what it means to love and serve other people.

Jesus taught that when we love and respect others, we show God how much we love him.

I want to be a servant for you, God.

... He dipped the piece of bread. Then he gave it to Judas, son of Simon Iscariot. As soon as Judas took the bread, Satan entered into him. So Jesus told him, "Do quickly what you are going to do."
—John 13:26–27

Day 318

Jesus always knows what is hidden in our hearts.

Jesus knew one of his helpers was not nice. One of his helpers was against him. This helper did not want Jesus to keep helping people. He wanted to get Jesus in trouble. Jesus knew who it was! He even shared his bread with the helper, a man named Judas.

Never let me hurt you with my actions or words, God.

Then Jesus said, "I am the bread of life. Whoever comes to me will never go hungry. And whoever believes in me will never be thirsty."
—John 6:35

Day 319

Jesus shared the Passover meal with his best friends. But this Passover meal was extra special. It was Jesus' last supper with his friends. Jesus held up the bread and told his friends that he was the bread that came down from heaven.

We need bread to live. Jesus is the Bread of Life!

Jesus, help me remember that you are the Bread of Life!

*Then he took the cup. He gave thanks and handed it to them.
He said, "All of you drink from it. This is my blood of the covenant.
It is poured out to forgive the sins of many people."
—Matthew 26:27–28*

Day 320

Jesus' life
was poured
out for us.

Jesus held up a cup of wine. He wanted his best friends to remember something important. He was giving up his life so people could have their sins forgiven and live with him in heaven. He told his friends to let the wine remind them of that.

You are the greatest gift, Lord.

Simon Peter asked him, "Lord, where are you going?" Jesus replied, "Where I am going you can't follow now. But you will follow me later."
—John 13:36

Day 321

Jesus told his disciples he would be leaving. He needed to go to heaven. He needed to prepare a wonderful new home in heaven for God's people. The disciples didn't want Jesus to leave. But Jesus promised he would come back.

God's Son was here on earth for a special reason. Then he went to heaven to prepare a place for us.

Thank you, Jesus, for preparing a place for me in heaven!

*"Do not let your hearts be troubled.
You believe in God. Believe in me also."*
—John 14:1

Day 322

**Jesus wants
us to be
joyful.**

Jesus said he was leaving. The disciples could not go with him. But Jesus did not want them to be sad. He did not want them to be scared. He wanted them to be happy. He said, "Soon you will understand, and you will be filled with joy."

Fill me with joy. Jesus.

Day 323

Judas was part of God's big plan. Judas was greedy. He went to leaders in Jerusalem. He knew they did not like Jesus. Judas knew how to get Jesus for them. He wanted them to pay for the information. The evil leaders gave Judas thirty pieces of silver.

God knows there are evil people in the world.

Help me to not be greedy, God!

He went a little farther. Then he fell with his face to the ground. He prayed, "My Father, if it is possible, take this cup of suffering away from me. But let what you want be done, not what I want."
—Matthew 26:39

Day 324

Jesus wanted his heavenly Father's will to be done more than his own will.

Jesus went to a garden. He talked to his heavenly Father. Jesus promised to do what God wanted, even though it would be very hard. Jesus prayed for strength. He loved all people. He wanted them to know God and to be able to go to heaven someday.

I want to be brave like Jesus!

"Do you think I can't ask my Father for help? He would send an army of more than 70,000 angels right away. But then how would the Scriptures come true? They say it must happen in this way."
—Matthew 26:53–54

Day 325

Judas took some soldiers to the garden. The soldiers arrested Jesus. Jesus' helpers were very upset! They wanted to save Jesus. But Jesus stopped them. He knew he had to go with the soldiers. It was part of his heavenly Father's plan.

Jesus followed his heavenly Father's plans even though he could have stopped them.

Help me follow your plans, God.

Then the high priest stood up. He asked Jesus, "Aren't you going to answer? What are these charges that these men are bringing against you?" But Jesus remained silent.
—Matthew 26:62–63

Day 326

Jesus trusted God, even when the soldiers and leaders were mean to him.

The soldiers took Jesus to the leaders. The leaders were looking for something to use against Jesus. So they made up false charges against him. Jesus could have defended himself. But he didn't He trusted God.

Jesus, help me trust you like you trust your Father.

The soldiers brought them to the place called The Skull.
There they nailed Jesus to the cross ... Jesus said, "Father,
forgive them. They don't know what they are doing."
—Luke 23:33–34

Day 327

The leaders were not nice. The soldiers guarding Jesus were mean. They hit Jesus. They made him carry a heavy cross. They nailed Jesus to the cross and Jesus died. Jesus could have stopped it at any time. But he didn't want to. It was all part of God's plan!

Jesus was brave and strong. He was willing to die because he loves us all so much.

Help me live a life worthy of your love, God.

Day 328

God's plans are sometimes hard for people who don't understand him.

Jesus was dead. People cried and were so sad. They were not sure what to do. Jesus had taught them about God. He had taught them about love. Jesus said he was going to die. He also said he would be back! But some people forgot what he said.

Help me trust you, God, even when I don't understand.

Day 329

Jesus' body was put in a tomb. Even though he was dead, the leaders were afraid of Jesus. they knew the people loved Jesus. They knew Jesus had said he would be back. They did not want Jesus' body to diappear! so they had the tomb guarded by soldiers.

No matter how hard people try, they cannot stop God's plans.

I am glad you are in charge of everything, God.

There was a powerful earthquake. An angel of the Lord came down from heaven. The angel went to the tomb. He rolled back the stone and sat on it. His body shone like lightning. His clothes were as white as snow.
—Matthew 28:2–3

Day 330

God has ways of surprising us!

Three days after Jesus died, the earth shook. An angel from heaven appeared! He scared the soldiers. They ran off. A big stone blocked the door to the tomb. The angel pushed the stone away. Then he sat on it.

Thank you for angels, God!

The angel said to the women, "Don't be afraid. I know that you are looking for Jesus, who was crucified. He is not here! He has risen, just as he said he would! Come and see the place where he was lying."
—Matthew 28:5–6

Day 331

Some women went to visit the tomb. They were Jesus' friends. They were very sad. They missed Jesus a lot. But they were in for a surprise! When they got there, they saw the angel. He said, "Jesus is gone. He is risen!" The tomb was empty!

> Jesus rose from the dead. He kept his promise!

Alleluia! Thank you for rising from the dead, Jesus.

Suddenly Jesus met them, "Greetings!" he said.
They came to him, took hold of his feet and worshiped him.
—Matthew 28:9

Day 332

Jesus loved his friends. He wanted to see them too.

The women ran to tell Peter and the other disciples that Jesus was risen from the dead! Then Jesus surprised the women. He was there in the road. The women could see he was alive! They were so happy! They bowed down and praised him.

I cannot wait to see you in person, Jesus!

On the evening of that first day of the week, the disciples were together. They had locked the doors because they were afraid of the Jewish leaders.
—John 20:19

Day 333

The disciples were scared. They knew the leaders did not like Jesus. They knew the leaders did not like them. It was not safe for the disciples to be outside. So they hid in a little room where they could all be together and pray together.

It is good to be with other believers.

Thank you for friends that believe in you, God.

Then he showed them his hands and his side. The disciples were very happy when they saw the Lord.
—John 20:20

Day 334

What Jesus promised the disciples came true! His promises to us will come true too.

The disciples were hiding together. Suddenly, Jesus appeared! He said, "Peace be with you!" The disciples could not believe their eyes! Jesus was back! He was alive! How could it be? They touched his hands and feet to be sure.

Lord, help me believe.

Again Jesus said, "May peace be with you! The Father has sent me. So now I am sending you."
—John 20:21

Day 335

Jesus had risen from the dead! There was great joy. The disciples were so happy. Now they knew that God loved them. Jesus was happy too. He prayed and blessed the disciples. He had a big job for them to do.

Jesus has big plans for us.

Jesus, I am ready to do my part.

"I'm going out to fish," Simon Peter told them. They said, "We'll go with you." So they went out and got into the boat. That night they didn't catch anything.
—John 21:3

Day 336

Don't forget about God when you go about your ordinary life. He can help.

After Jesus died, life could not completely stop for Jesus' helpers. They had to make a living. They had to get busy. One day, the men were fishing. They were not catching any fish. What could they do?

Lord, I will place my trust in you.

Early in the morning, Jesus stood on the shore. But the disciples did not realize that it was Jesus. He called out to them, "Friends, don't you have any fish?" "No," they answered.
—John 21:4–5

Day 337

The fishing was not going well. Then a man on the shore shouted, "Put your net back in the water. Put it in the water on the other side of the boat." Peter and his men did it. Then the net was full of fish! It was a miracle!

Jesus doesn't have to be in the boat with us to help us catch fish!

Help me remember that you can do anything, God!

Then the disciple Jesus loved said to Simon Peter, "It is the Lord!" As soon as Peter heard that, he put his coat on. He had taken it off earlier. Then he jumped into the water.
—John 21:7

Day 338

If we love Jesus, we should tell people all about him!

The net was full of fish! Peter was shocked. He knew the man on the shore had to be Jesus! So Peter jumped in the water. He swam to shore. He was right. It was Jesus! Jesus told Peter, "If you love me, take care of the people. Teach them about me."

Help me tell others about you, God

So you must go and make disciples of all nations. Baptize them in the name of the Father and of the Son and of the Holy Spirit. Teach them to obey everything I have commanded you. And you can be sure that I am always with you, to the very end." —Matthew 28:19–20

Day 339

After Jesus rose from the dead, he spent time with his disciples. He gave them a special job to do. He told them to go and make new disciples. He wanted them to teach others to obey God's commandments. He said he would always be in their hearts.

Jesus will always be with us. He will help us do work for him

Help me teach others about God's commandments, Jesus.

"I am going to send you what my Father has promised. But for now, stay in the city. Stay there until you have received power from heaven."
—Luke 24:49

Day 340

Jesus told his disciples what he wanted them to do. But he told them to wait for God's power.

Jesus was ready to go back to heaven. He had done his work on earth. Now it was time for his disciples to do his work on earth. Jesus said, "Go to Jerusalem. Wait there until you receive power from heaven. Then get busy!"

I need your power, God, to do your work.

But you will receive power when the Holy Spirit comes on you. Then you will tell people about me in Jerusalem, and in all Judea and Samaria. And you will even tell other people about me from one end of the earth to the other. —Acts 1:8

Day 341

Jesus was gone but the disciples did not forget him. They remembered things Jesus had taught them. Jesus told them to teach people all over the world about God's love. So the disciples talked and prayed. They made plans. They followed Jesus' example. They decided to teach others.

> **After Jesus went to heaven, the disciples remembered things he had said to them before.**

Help me be a good example of your love, God.

After Jesus said this, he was taken up to heaven.
The apostles watched until a cloud hid him from their sight.
—Acts 1:9

Day 342

The disciples saw Jesus go to heaven! It was more proof that Jesus is the Son of God.

The disciples had been with Jesus for three years. Jesus had said he would be going to heaven. But now it was time. Jesus promised that the Holy Spirit would come to help the disciples. Then Jesus went up to heaven! The disciples watched and were amazed. Jesus is the Son of God!

You are amazing, Jesus!

348

When the day of Pentecost came, all the believers gathered in one place. Suddenly a sound came from heaven. It was like a strong wind blowing. It filled the whole house where they were sitting.
—Acts 2:1–2

Day 343

Jesus' disciples were in a room in Jerusalem. Suddenly a big wind blew. It was the Holy Spirit! Tongues of fire came on the disciples. They could speak languages they had not known before! Now they could tell strangers from other places about God.

Jesus gave us the gift of the Holy Spirit to help us do God's work on earth.

Fill me with your Holy Spirit, God!

A crowd came together when they heard the sound. They were bewildered because each of them heard their own language being spoken.
—Acts 2:6

Day 344

God's Holy Spirit helps us share the love of Jesus with others.

There were many people visiting Jerusalem. Peter and the disciples got busy. They told everyone the Good News. They told people all about Jesus and his great love and sacrifice for the world. The people wanted to know Jesus too!

God, help me spread the good news to others.

Then Peter stood up with the 11 apostles. In a loud voice he spoke to the crowd. "My fellow Jews," he said, "let me explain this to you. All of you who live in Jerusalem, listen carefully to what I say."
—Acts 2:14

Day 345

Peter knew that Jesus wanted him to teach people about God after Jesus went to heaven. Peter loved Jesus very much. But Peter was a fisherman. He wasn't a teacher. So Peter trusted God to help him. After he received the gift of the Holy Spirit, Peter started teaching new believers!

> **Peter was an ordinary fisherman. But with the Holy Spirit, he became a great teacher of God's word!**

Help me to be a believer in your love, God.

Those who accepted his message were baptized.
About 3,000 people joined the believers that day.
—Acts 2:41

Day 346

It is a great day when people say, "I believe in Jesus!" Think about how happy Jesus is to hear it.

Peter and the disciples stayed busy. The Holy Spirit helped them. They talked to many people about Jesus. Three thousand people in Jerusalem said, "I believe in Jesus!" on one day. The disciples baptized each one of the new believers.

I believe in you, Jesus!

They shared their lives together. They ate and prayed together.
—Acts 2:42b

Day 347

As more and more people heard about Jesus, the church grew. The disciples taught so many people about Jesus. They taught about being baptized. They taught about sin. The people wanted to stay together to learn more. They prayed with and listened to the disciples. Every day, more people believed!

Jesus' followers prayed together. It is good to be part of a faith family.

It is good to be part of your family, God.

The believers studied what the apostles taught.
—Acts 2:42a

Day 348

Large groups of people wanted to learn about Jesus. The disciples worked hard to teach them.

The disciples taught the people. They lived with them and prayed with them. God had big plans for his people. God wanted them to know how much he loved them. Jesus' disciples kept teaching every day so more and more people knew about Jesus.

God, you never take a rest. You love me forever.

... Their hearts were glad and sincere. They praised God ...
—Acts 2:46–47

Day 349

Jesus' followers loved each other. They stayed together. They shared everything they had. They helped each other. They prayed and sang praise songs together. The disciples taught the followers about God and God's plans. Then the number of believers in Jesus grew and grew.

Jesus' followers sang praise songs together. He loves to hear our voices raised in praise and joy!

I will sing songs of praise!

They praised God. They were respected by all the people.
Every day the Lord added to their group those who were being saved.
—Acts 2:47

Day 350

The church of believers grew bigger and bigger. Think about how many people believe in God today!

The disciples did not rest. They told people all about Jesus. They taught the people about the Lord's Supper. The disciples told people about Jesus' great love and sacrifice. More and more people believed!

I believe in you, Jesus!

Peter said, "I don't have any silver or gold.
But I'll give you what I do have. In the name of
Jesus Christ of Nazareth, get up and walk."
—Acts 3:6

Day 351

Peter and John and all of Jesus' helpers were busy teaching. They met a man who could not walk. Peter did not have money to give him. He only had Jesus' message of love. Peter gave the poor man the message.

Jesus' love is for every single person.

God, there is nothing better than your message of love for me!

Day 352

Jesus' message of love gives people strength. That's one reason why we need to tell them.

It was a miracle! The man could walk! All Peter did was tell him about Jesus and his love! Other people were watching. They saw the man's joy. They knew it was because he heard about how much Jesus loved him. They wanted to know more about Jesus too.

Jesus, your love gives me strength!

*Meanwhile, Saul continued to oppose the
Lord's followers. He said they would be put to death.
—Acts 9:1*

Day 353

There was a mean man named Saul. He did not like people who believed in Jesus. He wanted them in jail. People were scared of Saul. They stayed out of his way. But Jesus was not afraid of Saul! Jesus loved him.

Some people do not believe in Jesus' love. God loves them anyway.

Help everyone to see how much Jesus loves them!

Saul got up from the ground.
He opened his eyes, but he couldn't see ...
—Acts 9:8

Day 354

Sometimes Jesus has to be tough on people. He really wants them to hear and understand his Word.

One day, Saul was on a road. A bright light flashed and he fell down. He heard Jesus' voice. Jesus wanted him to stop being mean to God's people. He wanted Saul to help people believe in Jesus. But, oh no! When Saul got up, he could not see. He was blind.

Please do not let me be blind to your message of love, God

For three days he was blind.
He didn't eat or drink anything.
—Acts 9:9

Day 355

Saul was blind for three days. During those three days Saul prayed, fasted, and thought hard about God. During that thinking and praying time, Saul realized that God had a special job for him. God's plan was for him to teach the world about God through traveling, preaching, and writing.

> While Saul was not able to see, he prayed. We do not need anything so big to start us thinking about God's love!

God, you know my talents. Use them for your glory.

Then Ananias went to the house and entered it. He placed his hands on Saul. "Brother Saul," he said, "you saw the Lord Jesus. He appeared to you on the road as you were coming here. He has sent me so that you will be able to see again. You will be filled with the Holy Spirit." —Acts 9:17

Day 356

Saul became an important helper for Jesus on earth. We can be important helpers too.

Saul needed help getting to a city. A man named Ananias was in the city. Jesus told Ananias to go to Saul. Ananias prayed for Saul to see. Then Ananias baptized Saul. The Holy Spirit was in Saul now! It was a new beginning for Saul, so God gave him a new name—Paul.

God, make me an important helper for you too!

*But Saul grew more and more powerful. The Jews living
in Damascus couldn't believe what was happening.
Saul proved to them that Jesus is the Messiah.
—Acts 9:22*

Day 357

Paul taught many, many people about Jesus. People who believed in Jesus were called Christians. Paul baptized these new Christians. He taught them everything he knew about Jesus. People were so happy to learn of Jesus' love and death for their sins.

> Paul made many new friends. Spreading Jesus' message is a good way to meet new people.

God, I am happy to be a Christian!

So Saul stayed with the believers. He moved about freely
in Jerusalem. He spoke boldly in the Lord's name
—Acts 9:28

Day 358

Paul spread God's
good news
around the world.
We can do that too!

Paul traveled all over the world. He walked for miles. He talked to many people. Paul helped the new Christians start new churches. Paul's new friends worshiped God. They loved Jesus and were happy to listen to Paul talk about Jesus.

God, help me tell people about Jesus wherever I go.

*While they were worshiping the Lord and fasting, the
Holy Spirit spoke, "Set apart Barnabas and Saul for me,"
he said. "I have appointed them to do special work."*
—Acts 13:2

Day 359

With the help of the Holy Spirit,
Paul became a great teacher. He
traveled to many places. He taught
many people. God even showed
people miracles through Paul!
These miracles helped even more
people believe in Jesus.

Paul traveled
near and far to
tell people all
about Jesus.

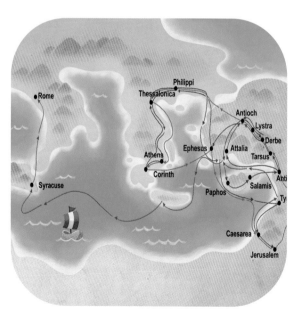

Holy Spirit, come into my heart.

About midnight Paul and Silas were praying. They were also singing hymns to God. The other prisoners were listening to them.
—Acts 16:25

Day 360

> God will help us whether we are doing big things or small things for him.

Paul and his friend Silas worked together. They taught people about Jesus. One time, some people who did not know about Jesus' love put Paul and Silas in jail. Other people might have been scared, but not Paul and Silas. They knew God would help them!

God, help me have faith like Paul and Silas did!

The jailer woke up. He saw that the prison doors were open. He pulled out his sword and was going to kill himself. He thought the prisoners had escaped.
—Acts 16:27

Day 361

Paul and Silas were in the jail. All of a sudden there was an earthquake! The doors flew open. Their chains fell off! The guard looked around. He was nervous. If the prisoners ran away, he would be in big trouble.

God takes care of those who love him. We can have faith that he will care for us.

God, thank you for rescuing your helpers.

The jailer brought them into his house. He set a meal in front of them. He and everyone who lived with him were filled with joy. They had become believers in God.
—Acts 16:34

Day 362

God sometimes uses tough situations to bring people to him!

Paul and Silas did not want the guard to get in trouble. Paul told the guard, "Do not worry. We are still here." The guard invited Paul and Silas to his house. When he and his family heard about Jesus' love, they wanted to be Christians too.

God, your message is good news for everyone who hears it!

John is a witness to everything he saw. What he saw is God's word and what Jesus Christ has said.
—Revelation 1:2

Day 363

One of Jesus' disciples was named John. When John was an old man, he had a vision. It was amazing! It was all about the future. In the vision, John even saw heaven! Jesus told John to write down what he saw in the vision and share it with God's people.

Jesus told his disciple John all about the future. God wants us to look forward to the future.

God, help me see heaven as clearly as John did!

Blessed is the one who reads out loud the words of this prophecy.
Blessed are those who hear it and think everything it says
is important. The time when these things will come true is near.
—Revelation 1:3

Day 364

Sometimes God tells people about the future. We can learn more about God's plans this way.

God talked to John. He blessed John with a special message about his coming. John was told to write down every word he heard and about everything he saw. And he did! The book of Revelation tells us about what will happen when Jesus comes for us again.

Help me to understand your plan better.

"'Here I am! I stand at the door and knock. If anyone hears my voice and opens the door, I will come in. I will eat with that person, and they will eat with me.'"
—Revelation 3:20

Day 365

We know that God is in heaven. But he is here with us too. He is with us all the time. Ask God to come live in your heart. He will do it! He will listen to your prayers and be there for you. Tell God you love him and are sorry for your sins. He wants to be close to you. He loves you.

God lives in heaven, but he will also live inside your heart if you ask.

Come into my heart, God!

The ABCs of Salvation

 A **A**ll people are sinners.

Romans 3:23
Everyone has sinned. No one measures up to God's glory.

 B The **B**ible is God's Word of love and salvation.

John 20:31
But these are written down so that you may believe that Jesus is the Messiah, the Son of God. If you believe this, you will have life because you belong to him.

 C The **C**ondition of sinners is serious.

2 Thessalonians 2:12
Many will not believe the truth. They will take pleasure in evil. They will be judged.

 D Christ **d**ied to save sinners.

Romans 5:8
But here is how God has shown his love for us. While we were still sinners, Christ died for us.

Everyone who believes will have eternal life.

John 3:16

"God loved the world so much that he gave his one and only Son. Anyone who believes in him will not die but will have eternal life."

You are saved through **f**aith.

Romans 1:17

The good news shows God's power to make people right with himself. God's power to be made right with him is given to the person who has faith. It happens by faith from beginning to end. It is written, "The one who is right with God will live by faith."

Good works will not save you.

Ephesians 2:8–9

God's grace has saved you because of your faith in Christ. Your salvation doesn't come from anything you do. It is God's gift. It is not based on anything you have done. No one can brag about earning it.

Hell and punishment are waiting for those who do not believe.

2 Thessalonians 1:8–9

He will punish those who don't know God. He will punish those who don't obey the good news about our Lord Jesus. They will be destroyed forever. They will be shut out of heaven. They will never see the glory of the Lord's strength.

I Nothing is **i**mpossible for God.

Luke 1:37

"Nothing is impossible with God."

J There is **j**oy in heaven over one sinner who repents.

Luke 15:10

"I tell you, it is the same in heaven. There is joy in heaven over one sinner who turns away from sin."

K If you trust God, he will **k**eep you from sin.

Jude 1:24

Give praise to the God who is able to keep you from falling into sin. He will bring you into his heavenly glory without any fault. He will bring you there with great joy.

L God **l**oves sinners and wants to save them.

John 3:16

"God loved the world so much that he gave his one and only Son. Anyone who believes in him will not die but will have eternal life."

M God has **m**ercy on unbelievers.

Romans 11:32

God has found everyone guilty of not obeying him.
So now he can have mercy on everyone.

N Jesus is the only **n**ame by which you can be saved.

Acts 4:12

"You can't be saved by believing in anyone else.
God has given people no other name under heaven
that will save them."

O You show God you love him by **O**beying his commandments.

1 John 5:3

In fact, here is what it means to love God. We love
him by obeying his commands. And his commands
are not hard to obey.

P God is **p**atient with unbelievers.

2 Peter 3:9

The Lord is not slow to keep his promise. He is not
slow in the way some people understand it. Instead,
he is patient with you. He doesn't want anyone to
be destroyed. Instead, he wants all people to turn
away from their sins.

Those who don't believe should quickly decide to follow Jesus.

2 Corinthians 6:2

He says,

"When I had mercy on you, I heard you.
On the day I saved you, I helped you."

I tell you, now is the time God has mercy. Now is the day
he saves.

 ## Christians have a reason to rejoice.

Luke 10:20

"But do not be glad when the evil spirits obey you.
Instead, be glad that your names are written in heaven."

 ## The Bible, the Scriptures, can teach you how to be Saved.

2 Timothy 3:15

You have known the Holy Scriptures ever since you were
a little child. They are able to teach you how to be saved
by believing in Christ Jesus.

 ## You should give thanks to God for the wonderful gift of salvation.

2 Corinthians 9:15

Let us give thanks to God for his gift.
It is so great that no one can tell
how wonderful it really is!

The Holy Spirit helps us **U**nderstand God's Word.

1 Corinthians 2:12

What we have received is not the spirit of the world. We have received the Spirit who is from God. The Spirit helps us understand what God has freely given us.

Jesus has gained **V**ictory over death for you.

1 Corinthians 15:54

In fact, that is going to happen. What does not last will be dressed with what lasts forever. What dies will be dressed with what does not die. Then what is written will come true. It says, "Death has been swallowed up. It has lost the battle."

Whoever calls on Jesus will be saved.

Acts 2:21

"'Everyone who calls on the name of the Lord will be saved.'"

God loves you so much he calls **Y**ou his child.

1 John 3:1

See what amazing love the Father has given us! Because of it we are called children of God. And that's what we really are! The world doesn't know us because it didn't know him.

**Building foundations of faith with
children for over 30 years!**

9780310750130
$19.99 / Hardcover

The Beginner's Bible® has been a favorite with young children
and their parents since its release in 1989 with over 25 million
products sold. While several updates have been made since
its early days, *The Beginner's Bible*® will continue to build a
foundation of faith in little ones for many more years to come.

Full of faith and fun, *The Beginner's Bible*® is a wonderful gift for
any child. The easy-to-read text and bright, full-color illustrations on
every page make it a perfect way to introduce young children to the
stories and characters of the Bible. With new vibrant three-dimensional
art and compelling text, more than 90 Bible stories come to life. Kids
ages 6 and under will enjoy the fun illustrations of Noah helping the
elephant onto the ark, Jonah praying inside the fish, and more, as they
discover *The Beginner's Bible*® just like millions of children before.

9780310768753
$24.99 / Hardcover

With the same beloved stories and illustrations of the original
The Beginner's Bible, The Beginner's Bible Gift Edition
makes the perfect read-aloud gift, with larger illustrations
and page size, ribbon marker, and a durable, yet attractive
foiled cover. A Bible to pass down or use everyday!

Bright and vibrant illustrations enhance every word, introducing
boys and girls to the timeless stories of the Bible and starting
them on a journey toward a lifelong love of God's Word. This
lovely keepsake edition of the beloved and trusted The Beginner's
Bible is the perfect gift for children ages 4–8 on baptisms,
dedications, birthdays, Christmas, Easter, and First Communion.
Give the children in your life one of the most beloved
storybooks of our time, and the perfect foundation for
their journey of faith, and a love of God's Word.

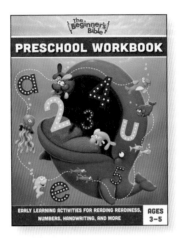

9780310751670
$9.99 / Softcover

Based on **The Beginner's Bible, The Beginner's Bible Preschool Workbook** is full of activities that will encourage young children ages 3 to 5 to grow in their faith and have fun while learning their letters and numbers. **The Beginner's Bible** has been a trusted illustrated Bible with young children and their parents for over thirty years.

The simple pencil-and-paper activities in The Beginner's Bible Preschool Workbook are based on classic Bible stories and characters such as Adam and Eve, Noah, the life of Jesus, and more.

Children ages 3 to 5 will enjoy over 200 pages of activities, including

- Handwriting exercises
- Letter and number activities
- Mazes
- Connect-the-dots
- Matching games

The children in your life will love working through the numerous activities designed to help them learn preschool skills while also learning about God's love for them, one Bible story at a time.

More products from *The Beginner's Bible*® to discover:

The Beginner's Bible
First 100 Bible Words
9780310766858

The Beginner's Bible
Learn Your Letters
9780310770244

The Beginner's Bible
All Aboard Noah's Ark
9780310768678

The Beginner's Bible
Little Lamb's Christmas
9780310770589

The Beginner's Bible Super
Girls of the Bible Sticker
and Activity Book
9780310751182

The Beginner's Bible
All About Jesus Sticker
and Activity Book
9780310746935

The Beginner's Bible
People of the Bible
9780310765035